THE PREPPER'S GUIDE TO FORAGING
SECOND EDITION

REVISED AND UPDATED

THE PREPPER'S GUIDE TO FORAGING

SECOND EDITION

REVISED AND UPDATED

HOW WILD PLANTS CAN SUPPLEMENT A SUSTAINABLE LIFESTYLE

DAVID NASH
FOREWORD BY TODD WALKER

Skyhorse Publishing

This book is dedicated to "Uncle Dan" Beard. His books on outdoor skills for boys led to long afternoons of outdoor adventuring and indoor daydreaming, and he inspired thousands of American boys, myself included. His books and my scouting experiences shaped the man I am today.

———————————————————————

Skyhorse Publishing books may be purchased in bulk at special discounts for sales promotion, corporate gifts, fund-raising, or educational purposes. Special editions can also be created to specifications. For details, contact the Special Sales Department, Skyhorse Publishing, 307 West 36th Street, 11th Floor, New York, NY 10018 or info@skyhorsepublishing.com.
Skyhorse® and Skyhorse Publishing® are registered trademarks of Skyhorse Publishing, Inc.®, a Delaware corporation.

Visit our website at www.skyhorsepublishing.com.

10 9 8 7 6 5 4 3 2 1

Library of Congress Cataloging-in-Publication Data is available on file.

Cover design by Tom Lau

Print ISBN: 978-1-5107-3772-3
Ebook ISBN: 978-1-5107-3775-4

Printed in China

TABLE OF CONTENTS

HOW THIS BOOK IS ORGANIZED

The first part of this book contains basic information needed to begin learning how to safely forage for and use wild plants. It includes a short introduction, addresses a popularly discussed universal edibility test, and suggests the best use of foraging. It also introduces the reader to commonly used plant parts and botanical descriptions and definitions to help identify plants. The second, longer, part of the book comprises a listing of 35 common plants and trees, their illustrated descriptions, range of habitat, and a description of at least one food and alternative use.

Wild strawberry plant. Courtesy of Arvind (CC BY-SA 3.0).

FOREWORD

When David Nash asked me to write an introduction to his book, I was extremely honored and excited. I'm a student who enjoys doing common-sense stuff to become more self-reliant.

I like the fact that he's actually doing the stuff in his books, as well as the no-nonsense style of his writing based in humility. His attitude is always that of a student, whether teaching about guns or plants.

Knowledge is not enough to get you and your family through hard times when fragile systems fail. As much as we'd all like to think that food trucks will always deliver, a small glitch (or a dusting of snow in Georgia) is all it takes for the industrial food machine to grind to a halt. Not a problem. You've got food put aside for such occasions . . . if the trucks start rolling soon.

What if they don't? I've read about many misguided people who plan to "live off the land" in the backwoods. That's not what this book is about. David puts that myth to rest right up front. Foraging from the landscape is a skill meant to supplement your overall food independence plan. But what many foraging books don't give you are alternative uses for wild plants . . . and trees are rarely mentioned. Trees, my friend, are a four-season meal plan!

The more I learn about the natural world, the more I realize just how little I know. There are hundreds of thousands of plant species in nature. In my pursuit of outdoor self-reliance skills, knowledge of the plant world is the foundation of becoming less dependent on others. I'm not a botanist but I do study plants and trees for their uses as food and medicine. However, one of the best value-added aspects of this book has to be the alternative uses of each of the twenty-five plants listed. That alone is worth the price.

David also provides some excellent resources to further your journey in wildcrafting. The common-sense advice to seek out a reputable plant forager is wise. Even then, you'll need to spend time in the woods or backyard practicing.

I would recommend locating and properly identifying two of the plants or trees each month. In one year's time, you'll have learned about twenty-four plants and their uses. That would be a huge leap in your journey to self-reliance!

Todd Walker

Todd Walker, a.k.a. The Survival Sherpa, is an experienced survivalist who runs several websites and Facebook groups dedicated to wilderness survival and bushcraft.

INTRODUCTION

As I wrote in the introduction to the first edition of the *Prepper's Guide to Foraging*, my childhood was deeply influenced by having a state park ranger as a father, and living in the middle of a large state park.

I spent countless happy hours as a boy reading old outdoor handbooks from the turn of the century, camping, and discovering for myself the rewards of being able to take care of myself.

My mentors and those experiences guided me and allowed me to develop the basic skills I use today as an author, experimenter, and self-reliance advocate.

With the positive reception of the original book, I took even more time to add plants, recipes, and projects. Also based on the audience, much of the medical references were removed to make room for more family-orientated projects. Almost without exception, any of the projects and recipes in this book could be completed by the average middle school aged child with a little parental supervision. That was done intentionally, as I find great satisfaction in sharing time with my son giving him the same gift of freedom to experiment and learn that my parents gave me.

Ostrich fern fiddleheads and wild leeks.

For me, books are a great way to learn and are fuel for the imagination, but in writing a book like this I am reminded of my favorite childhood hero, 15-year-old Sam Gribley from *My Side of the Mountain*. Sam hated living in a cramped city apartment, so he used his library card to learn survival skills and ran away to the mountains. He nearly gave up on his first night because books alone can't teach survival skills. Outdoor skills should be learned in the outdoors.

Before using plants found in the wild, please ensure they are the actual plants you are trying to eat. There are many plants that look alike; some are edible and some are not. I spent many hours learning these skills as a child, and many more ensuring this book correctly illustrates the plants, but I cannot guarantee that a photograph

Staghorn sumac shoots and fruit clusters from last year.

can correctly depict a live plant in the wild. Never rely on a single book to identify wild edibles, and if possible, always get advice from a local expert.

In my work as a professional emergency manager and a disaster preparedness educator, I constantly hear from people that planning to head for the hills and "live off the land" in a disaster. As we will discuss later, I just don't think this plan makes sense. There is simply not enough wild land available for everyone to go back to a hunter-gatherer lifestyle. For the casual outdoor enthusiast, planning to go adventuring and eat from nature's supermarket is a plan to go hungry. There is no guarantee that the food is in season, can be found in sufficient quantify, or is even growing in your area. However, having some knowledge and the ability to adapt can make your adventuring more fun and memorable. Being able to recognize sumac and make some refreshing lemonade to have with your camp meal is one example.

The Prepper's Guide to Foraging is not meant to be a plant guide or an exhaustive reference. This book does not have the space to cover all that information, and I don't have the time or resources to create a manual that exhaustively covers all the North American edible plants.

My goal is to create a blueprint to help you see what is possible when you are open to the idea that you can use wild plants to supplement a sustainable lifestyle. This would be a lifestyle where the majority of your family's food needs are addressed through a comprehensive plan that involves food storage and some manner of food production.

This book is designed to show how useful wild plants are. I choose plants that are easily identified, are edible, and have additional uses besides satisfying a growling stomach.

You may notice that the focus of this book is on trees. I am not biased against smaller life forms. However, as I chose the plants contained in this work, I made several conscious decisions that led me to a work that contained many trees. I will share two of them. The first reason that there are many trees selected is that many other books that deal solely with wild edibles focus on smaller plants and I wanted to share less common information. Another is that I believe that trees are both easier to identify and better suited to a lifestyle where wild food supplements, but doesn't replace, home-produced and stored foods.

Types of trees can be easier to identify.

Assortment of herbs.

HOW TO LEARN ABOUT WILD EDIBLE PLANTS

There are several ways to learn about wild foraged foods, but only two that are appropriate and safe.

THE BEST WAY TO LEARN ABOUT EDIBLE PLANTS

If you have access to a local expert, a real expert, not someone who read a book or two and started a YouTube channel, then the absolute best way to learn about wild plants is to take the time to study them with one. This process takes a long time, maybe even years, but you will learn the most information in the safest way possible. Going out into the woods with someone who can show you a plant, explain its habitat, and tell you about its uses, dangers, and methods of harvest is without a doubt the best way to safely learn.

I have a friend who is a master herbalist. They have a wild herb trail that they walk with students to identify plants in their wild habitat. When I have questions, I know right where to go. A good place to start for you may be a local naturalist or a nearby nature center may help.

When you have an expert show you a plant, you can smell it, taste it (if safe), and, most importantly, identify it in its natural surroundings. To put it another way, I can easily identify a tool by looking at a picture or seeing it lying on a bench alone, but it is much harder to identify the same tool when it's jumbled in among a full toolbox.

To be successful in foraging, you need to know a plant well enough so that you can skillfully hunt for a plant you have a particular need for, as well as quickly identify a food of opportunity when you stumble upon it in a time of need.

THE SECOND-BEST WAY

You can learn to identify plants through research.

I understand that not everyone has the time, ability, or personality to find and interact with an expert. It is hard to find someone who has the knowledge and is willing to invest the time and energy to share it with you. If you don't have access to an expert mentor, the next best way to safely learn is to spend the time to do the appropriate amount of research. This is probably the route most will have to take to learn about wild foods.

Do not rely solely on the Internet for your information. While I appreciate the power of the Internet, I do not use it for primary research when it comes to wild edible and medicinal plants, because quality control is nonexistent and mistakes can be fatal. It is very easy to create a website and present information, but it is much harder to present accurate information. The wide variety of Internet posts on attention-grabbing topics will attest that not everyone with a website cares about presenting factual information when they can get fast views. I recommend that the majority of the time you spend in researching wild food be done in a well-stocked library.

Traditionally published books tend to have a little better track record on information accuracy, but to go back to the tool analogy, it's easy to identify a single tool by a picture, but when looking for a specific wrench, would you trust your life to a single photo to pick a specific wrench from a pile of tools? A 13mm and ½-inch look almost identical by size. If I were going to eat a plant found in the wild, I would want pictures from several different books showing several different angles.

There is a list of useful books at the back of this one. However, just as with the Internet, don't limit yourself to a single plant identification guide either. The biggest problem I have with plant guides is that they just don't have a lot of pictures. If you are going to trust your life on the identification of a plant you found in a book, then do yourself a favor and cross-reference those pictures multiple times. Ensure that you check, cross-reference, and double-check your information as well as vetting the credentials of the author. Sometimes you can find a plant, but it isn't the best representation of the species.

HOW NOT TO LEARN ABOUT EDIBLE PLANTS

It's a bad idea to guess which plants are safe; poison ivy is safe for deer to eat, but **not** humans.

Guesstimating and improvising are two of my favorite skills when trying to get things done in a hurry. However, with some things (for example, moving heavy objects and eating wild things that can kill me) I force myself to go slow and work the right way.

As mentioned above, trusting only one source is a bad way to go. I prefer to gather five or more informational resources and vet them together to consider the totality of the facts before trusting my life to a piece of information.

Another way some people learn is to pick up a plant in the woods and try it without fully vetting it. Just because something looks like something you read about does not mean it is safe to eat. Many edible plants share characteristics with poisonous plants, which could lead to a painful experience up to and including death.

Playing fast and loose with wild plants—either for food or medicinal purposes—is very similar to Russian roulette. You can die the first time you make a mistake, or you may be able to make bad decisions a few times before you pay the price. The risk is not worth the reward when proper tools for identification are so easy to find.

For this book, I have chosen plants that are very readily identifiable and/or have very few plants that are comparable in looks. For example, it is very hard to misidentify a staghorn sumac with its red cone of berries or a sassafras tree with its three distinct leaf patterns, but please do not trust this book alone before you go out to the woods to try *any* of the projects or recipes in this book or any other. Cross-reference what you see with more than one other trusted source to ensure you always have accurate information.

Sassafras trees are easy to identify because there are three different shapes of leaves.

UNIVERSAL EDIBILITY TEST

Many discussions of foraging and wilderness survival will involve a mention of the "Universal Edibility Test." This test is supposed to allow a person to determine if they can safely eat a wild plant, but I agree with the opinions of many expert foragers who are against the use of this test. Many plants are extremely toxic, and consuming even a small amount will result in death. There are common plants so poisonous that you could take a bite of them in a hospital emergency department and die before you could be treated.

Upon studying the issue, I can't think of a situation where this test is worth it. In a wilderness survival situation that may come about by being lost in the woods, you are likely to be found before starvation occurs. Even in a long-term catastrophic disaster type situation, you should have time to research the plants before you eat them.

Therefore, do not eat any foraged wild plant unless you are 100 percent certain of the plant's identification and its edibility. Personally, while I find plant identification guides to be a vital part of my outdoor library, I take the additional step of getting identification of unknown plants from a local expert if I have any doubt about what I am looking at.

As I mentioned, the universal edibility test is controversial, especially because the United States Army includes this test in their survival manual. While this is true, I also know that the US military plays by averages, and they may be willing to take on the risk of a method that isn't 100 percent safe in order to prolong lives in an extreme survival situation. Most of us do not face army conditions, however, and should be much more careful.

With the above statements in mind, here is the most widely disseminated version of the edibility test follows.

The Universal Edibility Test is not necessarily universal.

UNIVERSAL EDIBILITY TEST

1. Do not eat for eight hours before performing the test so as not to involve food interactions. While fasting, test for contact poisoning by placing the plant inside your elbow or wrist for 15 minutes to test for a reaction.
2. Wash the plant.
3. Test only one part of the plant at a time.
4. Separate the plant into components—in some cases, one part of the plant may be edible but another toxic.
5. Smell the component for strong or acidic odors (smell alone does not indicate a plant is edible or inedible).
6. Place a small portion of the plant component on your lip to test for burning or itching.
7. Wait three minutes after touching your lip. If you have not had a reaction during the three minutes, place a piece on your tongue.
8. Hold the food on your tongue for 15 minutes.
9. If you have no reaction, chew and hold in your mouth for an additional 15 minutes. DO NOT swallow.
10. If you have not experienced any burning, itching, numbing, or other irritation after holding the chewed plant in your mouth for 15 minutes, swallow it.
11. Wait a further eight hours without eating or drinking anything other than purified water.

12. If you have no ill effects during the eight-hour waiting period, eat ¼ cup of the prepared plant component.
13. Wait another eight hours, taking nothing but water. If you have no ill effects, then the plant component tested may be considered safe.

Universal is a strong term, as this does *not* work universally. For what it is worth, the only time I would ever consider performing this test would be during a global catastrophic disaster in which I was dying of starvation and this was the only method of survival.

It would be helpful if I could provide both a section on the common characteristics of edible plants and some signs a plant may be toxic, as there is a common list of plant signs to avoid. However, these signs can be misleading, and a quick statement that all aggregate berries growing in North America are safe to eat is false (even if it is a commonly held belief). For example, Goldenseal has an aggregate berry, grows in North America, but is *not* edible.

The Goldenseal's berry is not edible.

PLANTS TO AVOID

While it is not possible to give a safe list of common characteristics of safe foods, I have a list of list of plant characteristics to avoid.

Do not eat plants that have:
- Milky or discolored sap
- Beans, bulbs, or seeds inside pods
- Bitter or soapy taste
- Spines, fine hairs, or thorns
- Dill-, carrot-, parsnip-, or parsley-like foliage
- Almond scent in woody parts and leaves
- Grain heads with pink, purplish, or black spurs
- Three-leaved growth pattern

While this is a good start, this list is contains misinformation, as several of the plants in this book have milky sap, taste bitter, or have fine hairs. No general list will keep you safe. You should rely on specific knowledge gained from reputable sources.

Since approximately 90 percent of wild plants in North America are inedible, it pays to be very careful with what you put in your mouth.

Thorns could be a sign that a plant is unsafe to eat.

The hunter-gatherer lifestyle isn't feasible.

3

IS FORAGING AN APPROPRIATE MEAL PLAN FOR OUTDOOR ADVENTURE?

Like all hard questions, the answer to this is a frustrating "It depends." While some die-hard mountain men (or women) will argue the point, there is simply not enough land to support the hunter-gatherer lifestyle.

In *The Economics of Subsistence Agriculture*, authors Colin Clark and M. R. Haswell claim that it takes approximately 98 acres (0.15 square miles) of ideal land to support a human being at the subsistence level. This is just one study, but it is on the conservative side of the issue, as various studies estimate that 10 to 700 square miles of land are needed to support a single person.

We only have 3,805,927 square miles of land in the United States (including the extremely large portions of the country unavailable for foraging). To that factor, in 2015 the US Census estimated 328,814,000 people living in the country; you can easily understand that we simply do not have enough land for any attempt at a society-wide hunter-gatherer lifestyle. My math shows that each American would have a 7.5-acre parcel using the numbers above. No matter the value of the land or how perfect it is for wild food growth, 7.5 acres per person is not enough to feed them using any type of hunter-gatherer lifestyle.

During the Great Depression, deer and turkey were hunted almost to extinction in large parts of the United States. Even with the scientific management of deer populations, enormous advances in hunting technology, and fewer hunters, many people who head to the woods to hunt are unable to harvest a deer. Imagine what it would be like to hunt in a forest full of hunters desperate to feed their families.

The math is clear that there is not enough land to use foraging as a means to gain food on a nationwide level, and even if there was, not everyone has the ability or opportunity to

Muscadine grapes.

forage as a main source of food. There are people who have the knowledge, skill, and access required to find wild food to eat, but they are generally wise enough not to rely on foraging as a sole means of food gathering.

If you have the ability to do so, foraging for wild food and raw materials is a highly appropriate means to supplement items carried into the woods. Foraging is a highly valuable skill, as all plants have some use, and the ability to identify and utilize them can come in very handy when the neighborhood big box store is closed.

I am familiar with the dominant plants on my land, and what uses I can get out of them. Having the knowledge of the plants in my area is vital to being able to supplement what I grow, buy, and store. Knowing what I need and what I don't have allows me to seek out seeds to plant perennials as a sort of food forest. The use of wise conservation and introducing appropriate wild plants into my property allows me to have what I need without having to spend a lot of energy in cultivation while still creating a sustainable supply chain that is just outside my front door.

The best way of summarizing all this is to quote from the famous wilderness expert Mors Kochanski: "The more you know, the less you carry." I bring my own food when camping, but if I can catch a fish or find some fresh muscadine grapes, then I have an even better meal. That is the mind-set I find most useful foraging for wild food.

4
IDENTIFYING PLANT PARTS

While I took great care not to get too technical in my descriptions of the common plants used in the second part of this book, you will need to have a working knowledge of the terminology if you want to be effective in researching wild plants. It is very hard to accurately describe plants without the ability to understand basic botanical definitions.

Knowing the correct terms will also identify you as someone who cares about the subject, which is vital in gaining the support of your local expert. I used to teach radiological response and had the same basic class I taught to cops, volunteer firemen, foresters, nurses, and doctors. When describing the symptoms of acute radiation sickness to laymen, I could get away with saying something like, "If you vomit within an hour of exposure you're probably going to die." But if I said the same thing (it did not matter if the statement is accurate) to a doctor, they would immediately label me as a novice or someone lacking knowledge. However, it would be different if I used the more technically accurate "Emesis within one hour of acute exposure is a positive sign that a lethal dose of radiation was received." It is the same with botany as it is in any other professional field; correct terms are more accurate and will yield a better result when talking among those in the field.

Here are some common terms organized into groups based upon stem, leaf, and flowers.

STEM PARTS

The term *stem* refers to the structure that provides support to the plant. It acts as both the skeleton and the circulatory system and connects the roots to the leaves and flowers. There can be either a single stem originating from the roots with lateral stems growing from it, many different stems coming out from the roots, or a combination of the two. Where there is just one stem coming from the roots of a woody perennial (tree), it is known as a *trunk*.

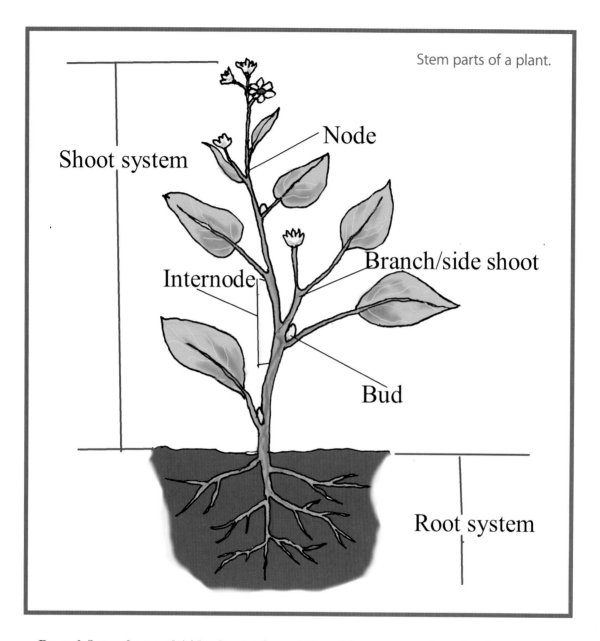

Stem parts of a plant.

Branch/lateral growth/side shoot: These different terms are used to describe stems that come out of the main stem. In general, they are slightly slimmer than the main stem or trunk of the plant.

Node: The node is the part of a plant stem from which one or more leaves emerge. Nodes often form a slight swelling or knob.

Internode: An internode is the area of a stem between two nodes.

Bud: A bud is an undeveloped or embryonic shoot. Buds most often occur at the tip of the stem or at the connection between leaf and stem.

Stipule: Stipules are small leaf-like appendages to a leaf, which are typically found in pairs at the base of the leaf stalk. Stipules come in a variety of forms, but not every plant has stipules.

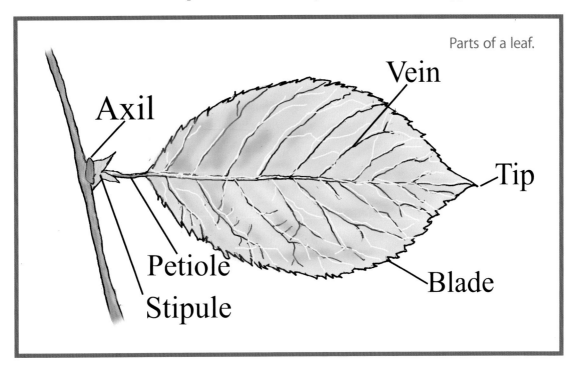

Parts of a leaf.

LEAF PARTS

Leaves grow out of nodes and are the organ of a plant that produces food. Oxygen and moisture are released from the leaf.

Axil: The axil is the connection between the leaf or leaf stem (petiole) and the stem or branch that supports the leaf.

Blade: The broad thin part of a leaf apart from the stalk is called the leaf blade (this may often be called a *lamina*).

Petiole: A petiole is the stalk-like portion of a plant that joins a leaf to a stem. It is generally flexible so the leaf can move in the wind, and some petioles will turn to orientate the lead blade toward the sun.

Sessile: *Sessile* is a term that describes a leaf that grows directly out of a stem without the benefit of a petiole.

Stipules: The stipules are two small flaps that grow at the base of the petiole of some plants. Some stipules, such as those of willows and certain cherry trees, produce substances that prevent insects from attacking the developing leaf.

LEAF TYPES

Leaves take on many shapes and are a vital part of plant identification. Most plant identification guides use these terms so that positive identification can be made:

Simple: Simple leaves are not divided or branched. Oaks, maples, and most deciduous trees have simple leaves of one leaf blade attached to a single petiole.

Compound: Compound leaves consist of two or more simple parts or individuals in combination. The blades of a compound leaf are fully subdivided into leaflets. A clover is an example of compound leaf, as is the black walnut.

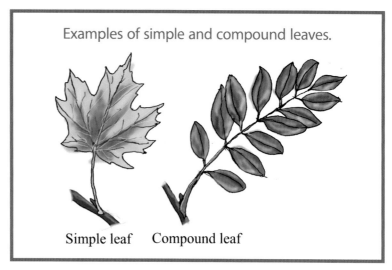

Examples of simple and compound leaves.

Simple leaf   Compound leaf

LEAF ARRANGEMENTS

Different terms are usually used to describe the arrangement of leaves on the stem:

Alternate: The leaves are placed alternately on the two sides of the stem. There will be only one leaf per node.

Opposite: In an opposite arrangement, there are two leaves per node. The leaves grow in opposed pairs, one on each side of the stem.

Spiral: In a spiral arrangement, there is one leaf per node, and it will generally corkscrew around the stem.

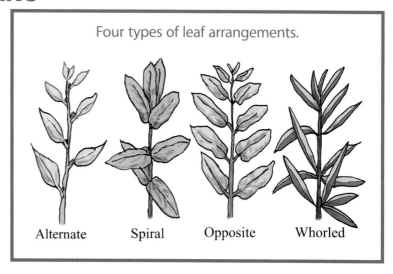

Four types of leaf arrangements.

Alternate   Spiral   Opposite   Whorled

Whorled: A whorled arrangement is a set of leaves, flowers, or branches springing from the stem at the same level and encircling it. There are three or more leaves per node. In the illustration nearby, four leaves arise from the same node.

FLOWER PARTS

Flowers are responsible for plant reproduction. This is where the seed, nut, berry, or drupe is formed. Flowers are very distinctive, and when present, greatly assist in positive plant identification.

Pedicel/peduncle: This is the stalk that supports the flower. Where this is a solitary flower, it is called a peduncle. Where there is a grouping of flowers, each flower is attached to a stalk called a pedicel. Pedicels are then attached to a peduncle, which attaches the group of flowers and pedicels to the plant.

Receptacle: The receptacle supports all parts of the flower and attaches them to the pedicel/peduncle.

Sepal: The sepals are small, petal-like structures

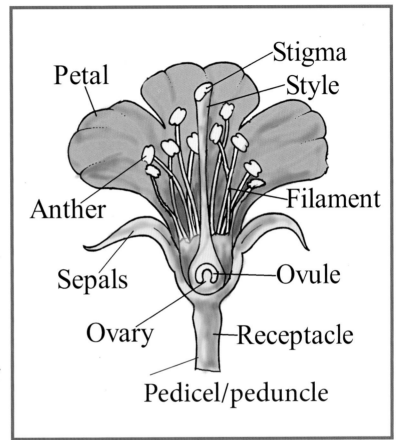

that sit below the petals and often form the covering of the flower when it is in bud form. They are often green and relatively thick. Collectively, these form the *calyx*.

Petals: Petals are the larger, usually colorful structures that surround the fertile parts of the flower. When the petals are brightly colored, it is usually to attract bees and other pollinators to the flower. Collectively, the petals form the *corolla*.

Tepal: Where the sepals and petals are fused into one structure it is called a tepal. In reality, a tepaled flower just looks like petals without sepals below them. Tulips are a common example of a plant with tepals.

Anther: The anther is the organ that produces the pollen sacs that will release pollen to fertilize the female ovule.

Filament: The filament is the stalk that supports the anthers and holds them at the right height to maximize opportunities for pollination.

Ovary: The ovary is the female portion of the flower that contains the ovule.

Ovule: The ovule contains the egg cells that will be fertilized by the male pollen. The ovule eventually develops into a seed and the ovary into a fruit.

Style: The style is the long structure that reaches from the ovary to the stigma. The pollen landing on the stigma must travel through the style to reach the ovary.

Stigma: The stigma is covered with a sticky substance that the pollen sticks to and feeds from before travelling down the style to fertilize the egg cell in the ovule.

TYPES OF FRUIT

There are many different end results to plant fertilization. All are developed to ensure that seeds become new plants. Fruits are divided into either fleshy fruits or dry fruits. Fleshy fruits are further subdivided by whether the fruit is formed by a single flower or a group of flowers. They can have one seed or several seeds in a group.

Berry, drupe, aggregation of drupes, pome, and hesperidium are types of fleshy fruits formed from a single flower, while sorosis, syconium, and coenocarpium are formed from a group of flowers.

Dry fruits are divided by whether or not the seeds are contained in a seedpod of some sort, or not. Seeds with seedpods are classified as dehiscent, while those without are called indehiscent. Dry dehiscent fruits are follicle, legume, silique, and capsule. Dry indehiscent fruits are achene, nut, samara, caryopsis.

Knowing the type of fruit a plant has might help you to identify it, and might also help you to know when the seeds and fruit are ready to harvest.

Berry: A single fleshy fruit without a stone, usually containing a number of seeds. Tomatoes are an example of a berry.

Drupe: A single fleshy fruit with a hard stone, which contains the single seed. A cherry or a peach is an example of a drupe.

Aggregation of Drupes: A fleshy fruit, made up of many drupes but formed from a single flower, each drupe containing one seed. A blackberry is an example of this.

Pome: A fleshy fruit with a thin skin that is not formed from the ovary. The seeds are contained in chambers in the center of the fruit. Apples are pomes.

Hesperidium: A berry with a tough, aromatic rind. Oranges, lemons, and limes are good examples of hesperidiums.

Pseudocarp: A pseudocarp is a false fruit, because it does not contain the seeds. The seeds are achenes, on the outside of a fleshy fruit. Strawberries are the best example of pseudocarps.

Follicle: A dry dehiscent fruit that splits on one side only. It may contain one or many seeds. The milkweed described later in this book is an example of a follicle.

Legume: A dry dehiscent pod that splits on two sides. Peas and peanuts are commonly known legumes.

Peanuts are a dry indehiscent fruit.

Silique: A dry dehiscent fruit that is long and thin, splits down the two long sides, and has a papery membrane (the septum) between the two halves. Cabbages and radishes are both silique seeds. A silique that is less than twice as long as broad is called a *silicula*.

Capsule: A dry fruit which splits open to release the seeds. It is the most common fruit type. Cotton, horse chestnut, jimson weed, and witch hazel are all well-known examples of capsules.

Achene: A single-seeded dry indehiscent fruit in which the seed coat is not part of the fruit coat. A sunflower has achene seeds.

Nut: A large single hardened achene. Chestnuts, acorns, hickory, and walnuts are all common nuts.

Caryopsis: A simple dry indehiscent fruit, like an achene, but with the seed coat fused with the fruit coat. Many caryopsis have been domesticated for food usage—corn, oats, rice, rye, and wheat are all examples of this.

Samara: An independent dry indehiscent fruit which has part of the fruit wall extended to form a wing. Maples are examples of this type of seed.

Always harvest sustainably.

RESPONSIBLE HARVESTING GUIDELINES

How and when you harvest plants have implications for use. As I sit at my computer writing this book, I have a set of gourds drying on a rack in my kitchen that were harvested over a two-day period—the first are drying perfectly, while those harvested on the second day are fighting mold growth. Knowing when to harvest is almost as important as knowing how to harvest.

GUIDELINES FOR PROPER HARVESTING AND STORAGE

While there may be specific plants that require different processing, here are some basic instructions:
- Harvest plants on a dry day.
- Harvest sustainably; do not take all of the best specimens of the plant species in an area.
- Keep harvested materials out of direct sunlight.
- Dry plants or use them quickly to reduce oxidation.
- Do not store plant materials if they are damp or they will mold.
- Take caution with plants growing near homes and occupied buildings or along roadsides, as they may have been sprayed with pesticides.
- Plants growing in contaminated water or in water containing *Giardia lamblia* or other parasites are contaminated themselves.
- Individual edible plants may contain toxic compounds due to genetic or environmental factors. One example of this is the foliage of the common chokecherry. Some chokecherry plants have high concentrations of deadly cyanide compounds, while others have low concentrations or none.
- Many valuable wild plants have high concentrations of oxalate compounds, also known as oxalic acid. Oxalates produce a sharp burning sensation in your mouth and throat and damage the kidneys. Baking, roasting, or drying usually destroys these oxalate crystals. An example of this is the Indian turnip bulb, which can be eaten only after removing these crystals by slow baking or drying the bulb.

GUIDELINES FOR ETHICAL FORAGING

As a responsible citizen, practice sustainable harvesting. Not only should you leave endangered plants alone, you should also never overharvest common plants in an area.

- Before collecting from the wild, consider using domestic or cultivated plants. Are there alternative plants that can be grown at home?
- Before harvesting, make sure you know your plant and are sure of its identity. Harvesting the wrong plant is wasteful and damaging to the environment.
- Know what species are at risk in your region. Never collect threatened, endangered, or sensitive plants.
- Only harvest what you need or can reasonably use. Overharvesting is wasteful and threatens the population.
- Scout around to see if there is more than one population. Check to see if there are signs of other people harvesting in the area. Find the healthiest population that doesn't appear to have been harvested.

Chokecherry.

Avoid removing the whole root of the plant.

- Be aware of the health of the environment. If the plants are stressed due to drought or other disturbance, don't harvest from them.
- To avoid overharvesting any one population, move around, collecting only a small amount of plant material from any one population.
- The rule of thumb is to harvest less than 5 percent of the population, less if harvest has occurred in the same area.
- Try not to disturb or compact soils where you are working. Leave the area as you found it. Always fill in any holes and step lightly.
- Leave healthy seed-producing plants in the population to reproduce.
- When you harvest plants, spread the seeds of the plant.
- Don't take the whole root of a plant. Replant root crowns of plants to ensure regeneration.
- Go back and monitor the effects of your harvest. Study the plants and how they respond.
- Always have permission from the property owner before you forage. As you forage and before you leave, do your best to leave no trace that you were there.

COMMON PLANT PARTS AND HOW TO HARVEST THEM

The individual parts of a plant have different properties and uses. The root of a plant may be deadly poisonous, while the flower may have therapeutic properties.

Flowers

Flowers are best harvested when fully open and after the morning dew has evaporated. Flowers damage easily, so be gentle. Cut the stem and harvest the flower whole. If the flowers are tiny, treat them as if they are seeds (see below). If the flower is large or very fleshy, pick the individual petals and dry separately.

Be careful not to overharvest.

Mint leaves.

Sunflower plant.

Leaves

Harvest and dry large leaves individually. Small leaves (like mint leaves) are best harvested and dried on the stem in bunches.

Seeds

I like to harvest a plant's entire seed head along with six inches or so of stalk. If you can catch the seeds just before they are totally ripe, you can prevent losing seed to birds or the wind. If you hang the seed head over a paper bag, the seeds will fall into the bag as they dry.

Sometimes, as with sunflowers, I will leave the flower on the plant and tie a paper bag around the still-growing flower. Then, once the seeds are ready, I can harvest them in the bag, which saves work.

Roots

Most (but not all) roots should be harvested in the fall when the above-ground plant has withered. Winter temperatures make digging difficult, so do not wait too long.

Aspen sap.

Do not use too much water when cleaning or wait too long to dry the root. Some roots will absorb moisture and might become soft and moldy.

Wash the dirt off of the root and chop large roots into small pieces while green. Hard, dry roots can be very difficult to chop, and I have experienced shooting bits of root around the kitchen while trying to chop very hard roots.

Sap and Resin

While the terms *sap* and *resin* are sometimes used interchangeably, they are two different things.

Sap is the plant's food and water. It is carried in the inner bark in the xylem and phloem cells and is composed of sugar and water as well as minerals, hormones, and other nutrients. Tree sap is sometimes drinkable and can be reduced to syrup. Later in the book, I will discuss how to harvest sycamore sap to drink, ferment, or make delicious sycamore syrup.

Resin is much thicker than sap, and is found in the outer tree bark layers. When a tree's bark is cut, resin is released to close the broken area, preventing the tree from becoming infected. I will show you how to use pine resin to make glue as well as a very bright torch.

Sunflower seeds.

THE PREPPER'S GUIDE TO FORAGING

Tree with bark harvested.

You can harvest both sap and resin in the fall when the sap is falling by either making a deep incision or drilling a hole and collecting sap in a cup attached to the tree.

Fruit
Harvest berries and other fruits before they are over-ripe. Discard any fruit with signs of mold. Damaged fruits can still be used in most circumstances.

Bark
Bark should be harvested in fall to minimize damage to the tree. Never girdle the tree by removing bark in a ring completely around the tree. Girdling will kill the tree. When American pioneers began farming a

Pine resin.

Willow bark.

Tulip bulbs.

new plot of land in a forest, they would begin by girdling trees to kill them so they could plant without the shade. In later years, the trees would be cut down.

Wipe down bark to remove moss, dirt, and insects. To dry, break bark into small pieces and lay flat on trays.

Bulbs

You should generally harvest bulbs after the above-ground leaves have wilted and turned brown. However, with plants like garlic, this will cause you to harvest loose bulbs that will not store well. Some bulbs need to be harvested when the leaves are still green. Either way, do not pull the bulb up by the leaves, but rather loosen the ground away from the root to allow the bulb to be harvested gently.

Wash, but do not use more water than necessary. Dry thoroughly without breaking the bulb. Something to consider when harvesting the bulbs of plants is that you will kill the plant. This means is it vitally necessary to take no more than one quarter to one third of the plants in a stand. When you are gathering bulbs for food, and the bulbs are small, consider a more sustainable food source, as it will not take long to decimate a population of plants in an area.

Wild ginseng plant.

TREES

Trees are often easier to identify than plants. They are also often overlooked by foragers and thought to be more of use as firewood or building materials.

Once a useful tree is found, it can be sustainably used over decades—which makes it a perfect option for those camping in the same areas over a period of years.

White pine (Mike Krebill).

Basswood leaf.

AMERICAN BASSWOOD

Scientific Name: *Tilia americana*

Type of Plant: Deciduous tree

Description: American basswood is a deciduous tree that grows to 60 to 130 feet tall and three to four feet in diameter. This tree grows faster than most other American hardwoods. The bark of the American basswood is smooth and gray to light brown, with narrow and well-defined fissures. Their twigs are smooth and reddish-green. Second-year twigs are light gray, turning dark brown or brownish gray in later years. The twigs are marked with dark, wart-like growths.

The leaves are long and broad, with unequal bases (the side nearest the branch is larger), alternately arranged, asymmetrical, coarsely serrated, and four to eight inches (but can get up to 10 inches) long. Fully-grown leaves are dark green in color and smooth, with shiny tops and pale undersides. The leaves have tufts of brown hairs, and are paler beneath with tufts of rusty brown hairs in the axils of the primary veins. The twigs and leaves both contain mucilaginous sap.

Basswood flowers.

Natural Range: American basswood ranges from Canada to North Carolina and westward through Tennessee and into Arkansas, the Dakotas, Nebraska, Kansas, and Northeast Oklahoma.
Food Usage: Both the leaves and flowers are edible, but the young leaves are tender and the best to eat. Bees pollinate the American basswood and create a popular light honey from its nectar. If you ever find basswood (also known as linden) honey, you may want to try it. Linden honey has a pleasing aftertaste that goes very well with breakfast teas, such as Earl Grey.
Basswood Salad: In spring and early summer, basswood leaves make a good salad green. The leaves have the sweetest flavor and tenderness when the buds have just opened. However, for several weeks into the growing season, the youngest leaves at the tips of new growth are suitable for eating. When the leaves are tough, they are too old for eating. You can also tell the youngest leaves because they are smaller, shinier, and lighter in color than more mature leaves.

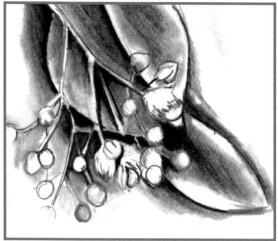

(Above) Basswood seed pod.
(Left) Basswood leaf and flower.

Basswood Syrup

Ingredients:
- 20–25 blossom clusters (fresh flowers work best)
- Juice and zest of 2 lemons
- 1½ pounds sugar
- ½ pound honey
- 1 quart water

Procedure:
1. Briefly rinse off the flower clusters. Discard the stems and wing-like bracts.
2. Place cleaned flowers in a large container. Add the lemon zest and juice.
3. In a small saucepan, bring the sugar, honey, and water to a boil, stirring to dissolve the sugar and honey.
4. Once the sugar and honey have completely dissolved, pour the liquid over the basswood flowers. Stir well.
5. Cover the container and leave at room temperature for 3–5 days.
6. Strain the syrup through a sieve or colander lined with cheesecloth. Transfer to clean glass jars or bottles.

Note: Syrup will keep in the refrigerator for a month. For longer storage at room temperature, bring the strained syrup to a boil. Pour into clean canning jars or bottles, leaving ½-inch of head space. Process in a boiling water bath for 10 minutes. Once sealed, the syrup will keep at room temperature for at least a year. You can use the basswood syrup fresh, yogurt, or cheesecake. Alternatively, add a small spoonful of basswood flower syrup to heavy cream before whipping it to make a flavored whipped cream.

BIRCH

Birch leaf with catkin (flowers).

Scientific Name: *Betula* is the genus name. There are 15 species native to North America.
Type of Plant: Deciduous tree
Description: Birch is a thin-leaved deciduous hardwood tree closely related to the beech and oak family. They are typically rather short-lived pioneer species widespread in the Northern Hemisphere.

The birch is a medium-sized tree, reaching 60 feet tall with a three-foot diameter trunk.

The bark is white, flakes off in horizontal strips, and the tree often has small black marks and scars.

In trees younger than five years, the bark appears brown, which makes it much harder to identify. The leaves are alternate, ovate, one to five inches long and two to four inches broad, with a serrated edge.

Birch
bark.

Natural Range: The birch is found worldwide and across North America.

The trees thrive in moist soil but require full sunlight. Birch trees have a shallow root system that make them susceptible to drought, so they prefer to grow in cool and damp enviroments.

Birches are often found in even-aged forest stands because they are pioneer species, and rapidly colonize open ground following a disturbance or fire.

Food Usage: The sap can be drunk similar to coconut water. Birch sap is easy to collect. Simply drill a hole into the trunk and lead the sap into a container with a tube or a thin twig, surface tension will cause the sap to follow the twig into a jar tied around the tree. Birch sap has to be collected in early spring before any green leaves have appeared as waiting longer will yield a bitter sap.

Birch Sap Syrup

Birch syrup is produced in the same way as maple syrup; you reduce the water content to concentrate the sugar content. But birch syrup is much more expensive, up to five times the price of maple syrup, since you get less syrup from birch sap. This is because there is about half as much sugar in birch sap compared to maple, so you need twice as much sap to make syrup. Depending on the species of birch, location, weather, and season, the birch sap will have about a 0.5 percent to 2 percent sugar content. You need about 375 to 400 gallons of sap to produce one gallon of syrup.

When making birch syrup, know that it is very easy to burn the sap because of the high fructose content, and it takes a long time to get rid of all that water.

Ingredients:

- 1 gallon birch sap (3–4 trees)

Procedure:

1. Boil sap down to half its original content in a pot—you can do this relatively quickly.
2. Transfer the ½ gallon of sap to a double boiler and carefully heat to remove the rest of the water until it reaches a thin consistency like maple syrup.

Birch leaf.

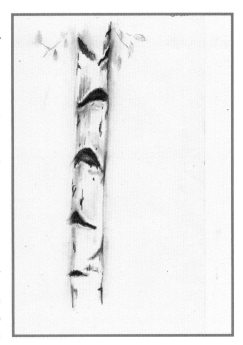

Birch bark.

Birch Beer

Ingredients:

- 1 gallon birch twigs, cut into small pieces
- 5 gallons water
- 8 pounds brown sugar
- 1 (2 oz.) yeast cake (or 3 packages active dry yeast)

Procedure:

1. Boil 4 gallons of water in a 5-gallon non-reactive pot. Add brown sugar, and stir until the sugar dissolves. Boil for 10 minutes. Add birch twigs and remove from heat.
2. When the water reaches close to room temperature (less than 100°F), stir in one cake of yeast (or 3 packages active dry yeast) dissolved in a half cup of warm water.
3. Cover and let it work for 10 days, or until the mixture clears. Bottle and cap tightly.

Alternative Usage: Tar for natural glue. The use of birch bark resin dates as far back as the Paleolithic era. It was used to seal boats and water containers and as waterproofing for shelters, an antibacterial covering for wounds, a flammable fire source, and a chewing gum.

Birch bark resin is useful, as it is solid at 65°F, but changes form as it heats.

- At 85°F, it can be molded in your hands.
- At 105°F, it acts as a putty.
- At 135°F, birch bark tar is a softer, sticky putty.
- At 352°F, it boils.

Unlike pine pitch, birch bark tar is not made from the sap of birch trees. Heating birch bark in an oven with little air is needed to extract the oil from birch bark. The birch bark oil will sweat out of the bark and run to the bottom of your oven.

Birch Bark Collection and Processing

Materials:

- 1-gallon paint can with lid
- Empty soup can
- Birch bark

Procedure:

1. Punch a hole in the center of the bottom of the paint can.
2. Trim birch bark so it is a little shorter than the paint can. Roll the bark together and insert the pieces in the can. When inserting the bark, be careful that you do not fill the can so full that you cover up the center hole.
3. Place lid on can and close it tightly.
4. Dig a hole deep enough so that you can insert your soup can. Your soup can should sit in the hole with the rim at ground level.
5. Place your soup can in the hole, making sure that it is stable and level.
6. Place the paint can over the soup can so that the hole in the bottom of the can sits over the center of the paint can. Make sure there are no air gaps between the two cans.

7. Use dirt to create a seal around the two cans to keep them together and to ensure nothing falls into the soup can.
8. Start a fire over and around the condensing can and keep it burning for an hour or so. The fire does not need to be large, but the paint can should glow a dull red.
9. Once the fire has burned down and cooled, scrape the dirt away, once again being careful not to allow dirt to fall into the soup can.
10. Your birch bark tar will be in the soup can.
11. To thicken the oil, slowly simmer it over a low heat for about an hour or so until it becomes quite gooey and is about half the original volume.

Notes: Birch foliage is used as a food by the larvae of a large number of butterflies and moths. Birch sawdust can be added to flour to extend it. The inner bark is edible and can be used as a flour substitute, but it will not rise. The wood of birches catches fire even if wet.

Birch bark. Courtesy of Thomas Drouault on Unsplash.

DOGWOOD

Dogwood leaf.

Scientific Name: *Cornus* is the genus name.
Type of Plant: Tree
Description: Dogwoods have simple, untoothed leaves with the veins curving distinctively as they approach the end of the leaves. Dogwood flowers have four parts. In many species, the flowers are borne separately in open (but often dense) clusters, while in various other species (such as the flowering dogwood), the flowers themselves are tightly clustered and are creamy-white with four petals each and appear in early spring. Dogwood trees grow 30 to 40 feet high and the fruit can be up to quarter-sized and look almost like single grapes.
Natural Range: Almost 60 species of dogwood trees grow throughout the United States, and the trees are commonly found in suburban yards. Dogwoods are most often found growing in forested, shady areas under other hardwoods and pines.

Dogwood flower.

Food Usage: The fruits of all dogwood species are drupes with one or two seeds, often brightly colored. The fruit of dogwoods is edible. However, some subspecies of dogwoods are very bitter because they contain tannins. *Cornus mas* and *Cornus kousa* are commonly used to make jam. The most common dogwood in America, the flowering dogwood, or *Cornus florida*, is not toxic, but it is very unpalatable—some say that is where the trees get their name—as being unfit for a dog to eat.

Dogwood jam.

Dogwood Jam
Ingredients:
- 4 packed cups dogwood fruit (*Cornus mas* variety works best)
- 1 cup water
- 7 cups sugar
- 1 packet SureJell
- ¼ teaspoon cinnamon
- ⅛ teaspoon freshly grated nutmeg

Tools:
- Canning jars, lids, and rings
- Saucepan
- Fine mesh strainer
- Blender or food processor

Dogwood flower.

Procedure:
1. Prepare the dogwood fruit (particularly the fruit from the *Cornus mas* plant) in batches by passing the whole fruit through a blender or food processor to roughly chop it and then pack it into a measuring cup. Repeat four times.
2. Set fruit and water to boil in a large saucepan over high heat.
3. Wash canning jars, lids, and rings with boiling water.
4. When fruit and water mix is at a boil, turn heat down.

Dogwood tree.

5. Measure sugar and SureJell together into a bowl, then sprinkle into fruit mixture while stirring.
6. Stir until sugar and SureJell are fully incorporated.
7. Add cinnamon and freshly grated nutmeg.
8. Simmer for 5 minutes.
9. Strain fruit mixture through fine mesh strainer into a large bowl. Press on the fruit solids to remove as much liquid as you can.
10. Ladle jelly liquid into canning jars. To further clarify the jelly, you can use cheesecloth or a fine mesh strainer as you ladle the liquid into the canning jars.
11. As you fill each jar, immediately wipe each jar rim with a cloth towel and twist the lids lightly into place. Wipe the jars down of any jelly liquid that has dripped on the outside. As the jars cool, gently tighten the lids. Some of the jars may seal by themselves. You will hear a pop and the lid will be sucked slightly into the top of the jar when it seals. If you want to be sure your jars seal, process in boiling water per directions on SureJell packet.
12. Cool on the counter for 30 minutes before storing.
13. Be sure to refrigerate until use any jars that do not seal.

Alternative Usage: Dogwood twigs can be used as a makeshift toothbrush.

Dogwood Toothbrush
Materials:
• Length of green dogwood twig approximately as thick as your pinky finger.
Procedure:
1. Peel off the bark.
2. Bite into green twig to flatten the end.
3. Use mashed end of twig to scrub your teeth.

Notes: Dogwood is fine-grained and hard. It can be used for specialty wood projects such as golf clubs, fine wood turning on lathes, tool handles, and cutting boards. Dogwood has also been used to make fruit presses. However, there is currently no market for commercial dogwood timber, so it must be harvested by the person that wants to build with it.

EASTERN RED CEDAR (JUNIPER)

Eastern red cedar tree.

Scientific Name: *Juniperus virginiana*
Type of Plant: Evergreen tree
Description: Red cedar is a dense, slow-growing coniferous evergreen tree that is ordinarily 16 to 66 feet tall, with a short trunk that is one to three feet in diameter. The bark is reddish-brown, fibrous, and peels off in narrow strips. The seed cones are less than ⅓ inch long.

The cones are dark purple-blue with a white wax cover. They contain one to three (rarely up to four) seeds. Thanks to its tolerance of heat,

Cedar leaves and cones.

Juniper leaves and berries.

salt, a wide range of soils, and other adverse conditions, the cedar can be put to good use on the farm in windbreaks and in city landscapes for hedges, screens, clumps, or even as specimen trees. It is an aromatic tree, with reddish wood giving off the scent of cedar chests and crushed fruit providing a whiff of the gin they once flavored.

Natural Range: The Eastern red cedar tree is common throughout the Plains States and Eastern United States. It is mostly found along roads, in fencerows, and scattered across abandoned fields. It especially prefers limestone soils.

Food Usage: The cones are used extensively as a flavoring, and while they can be eaten, their chemical properties make them too strong for routine consumption. However, the needles can be used to make an aromatic tea that has a slightly sweet and spicy flavor.

Juniper Needle Tea

Ingredients:
- 3 cups water
- ½ cup juniper needles
- Sugar and lemon to taste (optional)

Procedure:
1. Bring 3 cups of water to a boil in a saucepan or pot.
2. Add needles to water.
3. Reduce heat to a simmer and partially cover to minimize evaporation.
4. Continue simmering for 20 minutes.
5. Remove from heat and filter the needles by straining. The tea may be consumed warm or cold.

   Optional: Add lemon juice and sweetener of choice, such as maple syrup or stevia.

Alternative Usage: Several studies have shown that red cedar is useful for repelling ticks. One study even found it to be as effective as DEET.

Cedar branch.

Cedar Insect Repellent

Materials:
- Charcoal
- Dry cedar chips

Procedure:
1. Create a smudge by sprinkling dry cedar chips on a charcoal fire.
2. Let them smolder to create smoke that works well for repelling insects of all types.

Notes: The fine-grained heartwood is fragrant, very light, and very durable, even in contact with soil. Because of this rot resistance, the wood is used for fence posts. Moths avoid the wood, so it is used as lining for clothes chests and closets. If prepared properly, it makes excellent English longbows, flat bows, and Native American sinew-backed bows. The best portions of the heartwood are one of the few woods good for making pencils. Juniper oil is distilled from the wood, twigs, and leaves.

HONEY LOCUST

Honey locust leaves and seedpods.

Scientific Name: *Gleditsia triacanthos*
Type of Plant: Deciduous tree
Description: Honey locusts (also called thorny locust) commonly have thorns three to ten centimeters (one and a half to four inches) long growing out of the branches and trunks, some reaching lengths over 20 centimeters (eight inches); these may be single, or branched into several points, and commonly form dense clusters.

When young the thorns are fairly soft and green, but they harden and turn red as they age, then fade to ash grey and turn brittle when mature.

Locust trees can grow as high as 100 feet. They grow fast, but are relatively short-lived for trees, living 120 to 150 years.

The leaves are pinnately compound on older trees but bipinnately compound on vigorous young trees. The leaflets are five-eighths to one inch long and bright green. They turn yellow in the fall.

The strongly scented cream-colored flowers bloom in late spring, and form clusters emerging from the base of the leaf axils.

The fruit of the honey locust is a flat pod that matures in early autumn. The pods are generally between six and eight inches long. The sticky, sweet pulp inside the ripe, dark brown seedpod is edible, but has an acrid after-taste.

Natural Range: Native to Central North America, where it is mostly found in the moist soil of river valleys ranging from Southeastern South Dakota to New Orleans and Central Texas, and as far east as Eastern Massachusetts. The species has become a significant invasive weed in other regions of the world.

Food Usage: Honey locust is commonly thought of as a famine food, or alternative livestock fodder, but it is edible with work. As the recipe below suggests, it can be quite tasty if you have the time to process the seed pods.

Honey locust tree.

Honey Locust Pod Powder

Ingredients:
- A quantity of dry mature brown honey locust pods (brown but immature pods will taste bad, green pods are poisonous).

Procedure:
1. Boil a pot of water, remove from heat, and soak whole pods in water at least 4 hours, or overnight.
2. Split pods lengthwise and remove the seeds.
3. Break the deseeded pods up into small pieces. (you are not eating the seeds, but rather are using the *pods*.
4. Dehydrate the pod pieces. Use a dehydrator set on the medium setting (usually 135°F) or, alternatively, you can set your oven to its lowest setting (usually around 150°F).

Honey locust blossom.

Thorns on honey locust tree trunk.

5. Grind the dried pod pieces. An electric coffee grinder works, but so does a mortar and pestle. In my *52 Prepper Projects* book, I even used a length of pipe and a coffee can to grind flour.

The resulting ground mix is a sweet but gritty product that tastes sweet in baked goods and homemade energy bars. It does not work well in drinks, smoothies, custards, and other recipes in which grit is unsettling. You can sift your locust pod powder through a fine mesh strainer and use the finer mix for those things and use the trapped larger grains for baked brownies and the like.

Honey Locust Coffee (Tea)

This is more like a tea, but since the beans are roasted, I call it a coffee. This does not have caffeine.
Materials:
- About a cup of ripe honey locust beans (seeds) from a large grocery bag stuffed full of pods
- Cast iron skillet
- Grinder

Procedure:
1. Remove the ripe beans from the curly, dark brown seedpods.
2. Roast pods in a cast iron skillet until the seeds are dark colored. This should take around 15 minutes on medium–high. Stir as needed to prevent burning.
3. Cool seeds.
4. Grind into powder.
5. Brew as you would coffee. It will taste like English coffee, with a little sweetness.

Camp Brew Coffee Trick

If you cut the bottom off of a 20-ounce soda bottle, you can flip it over and insert the screw top end into the top of a glass bottle with a large neck (a thermos bottle works great). Put a coffee filter into the top of the soda bottle and fill with the appropriate amount of coffee. You can pour hot water into the filter and have coffee drip into your glass.

Notes: Honey locust is a great firewood. It burns hot and long, but be careful in a campfire, as it does tend to pop and throw sparks. It is also very rot resistant, and some farmers use honey locust and its sister black locust as fence posts. Some grow honey locust as a hedge and interplant it with Osage orange to make a thick and almost impenetrable thorny living fence (often called a fedge). It is said that the juice from the green seed pods is an antiseptic.

Camp brew trick.

OAK

Oak tree.

Scientific Name: *Quercus alba* (white oak)
Type of Plant: Deciduous tree
Description: There are approximately six hundred species of oaks. Oaks have spirally arranged leaves and some have serrated leaves or entire leaves with smooth edges. Oak produce an acorn nut that is edible, even though most species of oaks produce acorns with a high level of tannin, requiring processing before the acorn is palatable.
Natural Range: Oak trees are native to the Northern Hemisphere, and include deciduous and evergreen species that are widely disbursed in North, Central, and South Americas, Asia, Europe, and North Africa. There are over 90 different types of oak trees in the United States alone.

Food Usage: Acorns are edible, but many acorns need to be processed to remove the bitter tasting tannin compound from the nuts. In *52 Prepper Projects*, I showed how to process the nuts and use them as a flour substitute. The process is simple. Remove the nutmeat from the shell by breaking the hard outer coating and picking the nutmeat out. Then soak the nut in water for several hours. When the water takes on a dark color, pour it off and replace the water. Do this until the water is clear or the nuts taste palatable to you. This slow leaching of whole acorns may require a week of effort. Once the acorns are leached, they can be dried to grind into flour or used while the chunks are still damp.

Roasted Acorns

Ingredients:
- Leached Acorns
- Salt

Procedure:
1. Place the damp nut chunks on a baking sheet and sprinkle with salt.
2. Toast them for 15–20 minutes at 375°F in an oven.
3. The nuts are ready when the color has darkened slightly and the nut pieces smell like roasted nuts.

Oak leaves with acorns.

Alternative Usage: The tannic acid removed from the acorns (or harvested from oak wood bark and chips) can be used to vegetable-tan leather.

Vegetable-Tanned Hide

Materials:
- 30 gallons tannic acid (dark water gathered from boiling acorns, oak bark, and oak chips)
- 4-pound bag of hydrated lime (garden stores sell this, but I have an article on my tngun. com website showing how to make this from limestone)
- 5 gallons fresh chicken or cow manure
- Water
- 100 percent neatsfoot oil
- Small piece of beeswax

Procedure:
1. The flesh side of the hide is scraped with a dull knife to remove any traces of flesh, blood, and fat.
2. Once the hide has been thoroughly scraped, wash it off.
3. Put approximately 15 gallons of water in a large plastic garbage can.
4. Mix in hydrated lime and stir well.
5. Put the hide in the liquid and churn for two or three days. The hair will start slipping out of the hide when the hide is ready.
6. Remove the hide and scrape the hair side to remove the hair.
7. Rinse hide in a plastic tub with eight or nine changes of water.
8. Mix manure with enough water to make a medium slurry. Mix slurry and the hide in the plastic tub.
9. Stir the hide constantly for 30 minutes and let set for another three or four days with occasional stirring.
10. This manure process is called bating, and it makes the hide soft. When the bating process is done, rinse the hide very well using 12 or 13 changes of water and scrape both sides until the hide is clean and smooth.
11. Place the hide in the tub filled with the tannic acid bath, stir for 15 minutes, and let sit for a week, stirring every few hours. If the mix starts to ferment with sulfur-like smell, dump a half gallon of white vinegar into the mix.
12. After three weeks, dump out the mix and refresh with more tannic acid. Repeat the process for an additional six weeks.
13. Repeat the process with a very strong and dark tannic acid bath and let the leather sit for three months.
14. Take the leather out of the vat and rinse twelve or more times in clean water.
15. Place the hide on a hard surface and use a piece of smooth hard wood to squeegee out the water, but do not let it dry.

Oak acorn.

Oak leaf.

16. Heat up 100 percent pure neatsfoot oil and melt some beeswax into it.
17. Let cool and work it deeply into the hair side of the hide.
18. Flip it over and let the hide slowly dry over a couple of days.
19. Occasionally work the leather by pulling and stretching it.
20. Once dry, dampen the leather slightly and warm your oil and beeswax mix and rub it into the flesh side of the leather.
21. Work the leather as it dries and when done, you will have leather tanned much like the leather of the American pioneers.

Notes: Not all acorns require leaching of tannin. Native American Indian tribes have fought wars over sweet oaks that were especially prolific, as an oak can produce thousands of acorns, with an acre of oak trees producing more than a quarter ton of nutmeat.

OSAGE ORANGE

Osage orange tree.

Scientific Name: *Maclura pomifera*
Type of Plant: Deciduous tree
Description: This tree grows from 30 to 50 feet tall, but can be much shorter if grown as a natural barrier and routinely trimmed. It has a distinctive fruit that is roughly spherical, bumpy, and three to five inches in diameter.

Natural Range: The natural range of this ancient tree was a small area of Texas, Oklahoma, and Arkansas—the drainage basin of the Red River. However, farmers made very secure living fences by growing the thorny, rot-resistant wood in very tight rows, so it is found throughout the United States

Food Usage: This plant is often labeled as inedible, as the sticky latex sap can cause dermatitis, and makes accessing the seeds extremely difficult. It is edible, but is best considered to be a survival food, as often the seeds aren't worth gathering. Squirrels do tend to love the seeds, especially after the seed balls have rotted a little, making access easier.

Roasted Osage Orange Seeds

Ingredients:
- Osage orange seed ball
- Water
- Salt

Procedure:
1. Cut the ball in half and soak in a bucket of water until the latex (white material around seeds) loosens its hold of the seeds.
2. Use gloves to pull the seeds from the ball.
3. Preheat oven to 300°F.
4. Toss seeds in a bowl with salt.
5. Spread the seeds in a single layer on a baking sheet
6. Bake for about 45 minutes or until golden brown, stirring occasionally.

Alternative Usage: Osage orange (also known as hedge balls) makes a very nice natural dye. Colors vary between yellow, orange, and gold depending on amount of wood used, time soaked, and the fiber used.

(Above) Osage orange leaf.
(Left) Osage orange seeds.
(Far left) Osage orange tree.

Osage orange
seed ball.

Osage Orange Dye

Materials:

- Approximately 4 ounces Osage orange wood chips per pound of fiber to be dyed
- Water
- Fiber

Procedure:

1. Boil water and Osage orange wood chips for at least 30 minutes.
2. Let the pot cool to touch and strain wood chips/shavings from the pot.
3. Evenly soak fibers in hot water before placing them in the dyebath.
4. Reheat dye water while soaking fibers in the hot clean water.
5. Place wet fibers into the dye.
6. Boil fibers and dye at a slow boil for approximately 1 hour. Use a stick to keep the fiber submerged and free of air bubbles. Don't put too much fiber in the pot or you will end up with a splotchy dye job.
7. Reduce heat and let the fibers cool in the dye. Longer soaks make stronger colors.
8. Remove the fibers from dyebath.
9. Rinse with cold water until water runs clear.
10. Hang to dry.

Notes: Several articles on the Internet contend that Osage orange are a good insect repellent. While studies show the fruit does contain a small amount of a chemical insect repellent, it is not a high concentration and in practice it does not seem to work well.

SASSAFRAS

Sassafras leaves (all three shapes).

Scientific Name: *Sassafras albidum*
Type of Plant: Deciduous tree
Description: Sassafras is one of the first trees I learned to identify as a child growing up as the son of a state park ranger. I found the sassafras easy to identify because it has three different leaf patterns. It has an oval leaf, a mitten-shaped leaf, and a three-pronged leaf. This makes it almost impossible to misidentify. The sassafras tree grows 30 to 115 feet tall, with upswept branches and twigs. Saplings have green bark. The young leaves and twigs produce a citrus scent when crushed.
Natural Range: Sassafras ranges from Southern Maine and Southern Ontario west to Iowa, and south to Central Florida and Eastern Texas. It is most often found in open woods, along fencerows, or in fields. It thrives in moist, well-drained, or sandy loam soils and tolerates a variety of soil types.
Food Usage: If you have ever eaten filé gumbo, you have eaten sassafras. While okra is used as a thickening agent in traditional Louisiana gumbo, okra does not keep well, so filé powder made from dried, powdered sassafras leaves is used instead. I personally like filé gumbo better.

Sassafras fruit.

Filé gumbo.

Filé Powder

Ingredients:
- Sassafras
- Bay leaf (optional)

Procedure:
1. Locate a sassafras tree and cut several branches containing young, tender leaves.
2. Hang the branches outside, out of direct sunlight, for a week or until dry.
3. When the leaves are completely dry, remove the leaves from the stems.
4. Pulverize leaves (including optional bay leaf) with a mortar and pestle until very finely powdered.
5. Pass the powder through a very fine sieve.
6. Store in an airtight container and keep out of the sunlight.
7. Use sparingly, as too much filé in your gumbo will turn it to thick sludge. Also, you should wait to add it in the last few minutes of the cooking process, as too much heat will make it bitter and unappetizing.

Filé Gumbo

Ingredients:
- Vegetable oil
- 4 (3-pound) chickens, cut into small chunks
- 1 cup all-purpose flour
- 1 cup butter
- 2 each red, green, and yellow bell peppers, chopped
- 1 large yellow onion, chopped
- 1½ tablespoons minced garlic
- 3 tablespoons chopped parsley leaves
- 5 teaspoons salt
- 2 teaspoons black pepper
- 1 teaspoon cayenne pepper
- 5 bay leaves
- 2½ teaspoons dried thyme
- 3½ quarts water
- 2 links Andouille sausage, cut into ¼-inch half circles
- ¾ pound ham, cut into ¼-inch chunks
- 1 pound small shrimp, cleaned and deveined
- ½ pound okra
- 5 tablespoons filé powder

Sassafras flower.

Procedure:
1. Heat oil in a large stockpot over medium-high heat and cook the chicken until it is golden brown. Remove and set aside.
2. Add the flour to the chicken juices and stir continuously. Add the butter and cook the roux until it is brown.
3. Add peppers, onion, garlic, parsley, salt, black pepper, cayenne, bay leaves, thyme, and 1 quart water. Stir well and bring to a boil.
4. When the vegetables are soft, return the chicken to the pot and add the remaining water.
5. In a skillet over medium heat, cook sausage and ham until browned. Add the cooked sausage and ham to the stewpot along with the shrimp and stir well. Let the gumbo simmer for 1 hour
6. Add okra. Simmer 20 minutes, and then turn off the heat.
7. Ladle a couple of cups of the liquid into a mixing bowl. Add the filé powder and whisk until well blended. Pour back into the stockpot and mix well. Serve.

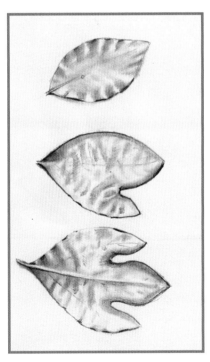

Sassafras leaves.

STAGHORN SUMAC

Staghorn sumac thicket with red fruit heads.

Scientific Name: *Rhus typhina*
Type of Plant: Deciduous shrub or small tree
Description: Sumac is a deciduous shrub or small tree growing to 15 feet tall. It has alternate, pinnately compound leaves 10 to 22 inches long, with 9 to 31 serrate leaflets each. The stalk that attaches the leaf blade to the stem is densely covered in rust-colored hairs. Staghorn sumac is most easily identified by its fruit, which sits in dense clusters of small red drupes at the end of the branches. These clusters are conical, four to eight inches long, and approximately two inches across at the base. The plant flowers from May to July and fruit ripens from June to September. The fruit has been known to last through winter and into spring.

IMPORTANT: Staghorn sumac is not to be confused with poison sumac. Non-poisonous sumac has red drupes. Green or dirty white drupes are from the poisonous variety and should not be used.

Natural Range: Staghorn sumac is found mostly in the Eastern United States. It is a common sight along highways and rural routes throughout the Southern United States.

Food Usage: Sumac is best known for a tart tea made from soaking the drupes in cold water. This drink is thought to be high in vitamin C and is a nice summertime treat. Sumac is used as a flavoring in many Middle Eastern regions. Gently grating sumac drupes creates a spice that has a tangy flavor that is similar to, but less tart than, lemon juice. It's best sprinkled over foods before serving, but can be used in marinades and dressings. While it is great over vegetables and hummus, it really shines when used on meat.

Staghorn sumac drupe cluster.

Sumac Dry Rub

Ingredients:
- 5 tablespoons sea salt
- 4 tablespoons black pepper
- 2 tablespoons gently grated sumac drupes
- 2 tablespoons garlic powder
- 2 tablespoons ground coffee
- 1 tablespoon cocoa powder
- 1 tablespoon brown sugar

Procedure:
1. Mix ingredients well to make one cup of rub. You will need approximately ¼ cup of rub mix per steak.
2. Apply a generous amount of rub to one side of steak. Using your hand, rub the spices into the meat until it is fully covered. Turn steak over and repeat.
3. Cover the meat and let it rest in the refrigerator overnight.

Staghorn sumac leaf.

Close-up of staghorn sumac's fuzzy fruit head.

4. Let the meat reach room temperature prior to grilling it. Put the steaks on a preheated grill and cook to your taste.

Alternative Usage:
Sumac is used as a dye as well as a natural mordant. A mordant sets dyes in the fabric so that they do not wash out. While you should always test a small scrap of the fabric before using natural plant dyes so you won't be surprised, the following recipe should produce a nice burgundy color when used with 100 percent cotton.

Staghorn sumac spice.

Sumac Dye
Ingredients:
- 2 gallons sumac drupes
- Water
- Cotton

Procedure:
1. Cover the berries with 1 gallon of water and boil for an hour.
2. When dye is desired strength, strain dye thoroughly, because any loose berries will cause a dark patch on the cloth.
3. Immerse cotton, adding more water if necessary.
4. Boil for at least 30 minutes and until fabric is desired shade.
5. Rinse in cold water.
6. Dry.

Be aware that an ingredient in modern detergents causes sumac-dyed fabric to change color to a grayish green, so wash with water only after you test the soap first.

Notes: Some beekeepers use dried sumac bobs as a source of fuel for their smokers

Sycamore tree.

SYCAMORE

Scientific Name: *Platanus occidentalis*

Type of Plant: Deciduous tree

Description: Sycamores are easy to identify because the bark flakes off in large irregular masses. This molting causes the tree trunk to have a mottled look with splotches of greenish-white, gray, and brown. A sycamore can grow to 100 to 160 feet high and five to six and a half feet in diameter. The sycamore tree often divides near the ground into several trunks, and the trunks of large trees are often hollow.

Natural Range: The sycamore often grows near rivers and in wetland areas. Its native range is quite extensive in the United States including throughout the Eastern US and Midwest. Because it is sometimes grown for timber, it has been planted outside its native range.

Food Usage: While not as familiar to most as maple sugaring, the process of collecting

Sycamore leaf and seed balls.

sycamore sap has been known for hundreds of years. It is very easy to collect. Sycamore sap can be drunk straight from the collection can, fermented into a drink, or condensed down into syrup. A healthy sycamore produces one gallon of sap per day at the height of the sap run, and the season is generally a month long. Sap flows best on days that are above freezing following nights during which the temperature had dropped below freezing. When deciding what to do with your sap, note that it takes 10 gallons of sap to condense into a quart of syrup. You will need 10 or more trees to gather any appreciable amount, but it is a fairly easy process.

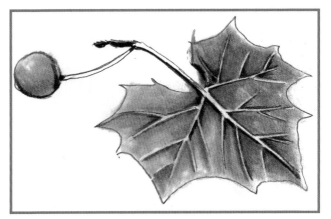

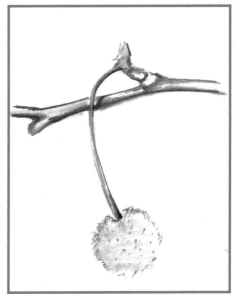

(Top) Sycamore leaf.
(Above) Sycamore seed ball.

Collecting Sycamore Sap

Materials:
- Drill and 7/16-drill bit
- ½-inch vinyl tubing
- Collection jugs (water jugs are fine, but thicker plastic is better as long as it is food safe)

Procedure:
1. Find sycamores at least one foot in diameter. Large trees can hold more than one tap, but sometimes the tree is more productive with fewer taps. Too many taps can potentially damage the tree.
2. Drill a hole three inches deep on the south side of each tree.
3. Angle your bit slightly upward as you drill to encourage the sap to drain.
4. Clean out each drill hole to remove any shavings.
5. Insert one end of the tubing into the hole and the other end into the container.
6. Collect your sap each day to avoid overflowing containers.

Condensing Sycamore Syrup

Ingredients:
- Steady heat source (a wood fire is fine, but I prefer a propane fryer)
- Large pot
- Plenty of sap

Procedure:

1. Do this project outside, as you will be boiling the water from the sap, which will cause condensation.
2. Bring the sap to a boil and keep it boiling until it visibly thickens.
3. Dip a spoon into the syrup and pull out one spoonful.
4. Allow it to cool for a moment and then see how it pours. If the syrup forms a curtain-like sheet off the spoon edge, then you are done. If it is runny, keep boiling.
5. Keep your finished syrup refrigerated or can in a water bath canner for longer storage.

Alternative Usage: Sycamore is not the best wood for many types of woodworking projects as it is coarse-grained and difficult to work with, but when carved green, it has been used extensively for butcher blocks and food utensils. Sycamore is a readily available wood and perfect when green for spoons. When dry or nearly dry it can be very hard, so it is best to do the carving, especially the roughing out, while green.

Spoon carving.

Tips for Spoon-Carving

- Always make sure you use a maximum of half, but preferably only a quarter, of the log or less. This reduces splitting problems.
- Make sure not to include the pith in any part of your carving.
- Be careful not to make the neck of the spoon too thin.
- Leave your spoon block in water when done for the day.
- Once a spoon is carved, just let it dry. It is not necessary to wrap it in anything. Do not dry rapidly or subject to heat while drying.
- If you need to keep the spoon green, either leave in a plastic bag or place it in the freezer.

Carving a Spoon

1. Draw the top profile of your spoon on a block of wood—the grain should run along the long end.
2. Remove as much wood as possible from the block to come close to your drawn edge.
3. Using a sharp knife, carefully carve right to your line all the way around the block.
4. Sketch the side profile of your spoon on the block.
5. Using a sharp knife, remove wood to match your design.
6. If you have a crooked knife, you probably don't need a tutorial, but if you want to buy one it makes it simple to carve out the bowl of the spoon. Use your thumb and finger to judge thickness of the bowl and go slow so you do not carve a hole through it.
7. If you cannot or don't want to buy a hook knife, you can cheat and use a small burning ember to slowly burn away a depression. Go slowly and carefully, as too much heat can cause your wood to crack. I have used this process to make spoon bowls. Simply set a glowing ember on the wood you wish to char away and blow on it through a metal straw (a small piece of copper tube is the easiest to use). As the wood chars, scrape it away with a knife or a piece of glass.
8. Once the bowl is carved, sand the spoon smooth.
9. Let dry.
10. Coat the spoon with edible oil such as olive or walnut oil.

Notes: Sycamore is a good wood to use as a wood drill when lighting a fire by friction. It also works well as firewood as it produces a hot flame and strong embers.

WALNUT

Walnut and leaves.

Scientific Name: *Juglans* is the genus. The eastern black walnut (*Juglans nigra*) is a common species in North America.

Type of Plant: Deciduous tree

Description: Walnut trees have a wide-spreading canopy. The trunk of the tree can reach over six and a half feet in diameter and 160 feet in height. Mature walnut trees have a dark, grayish-brown bark with interlacing ridges. Its bright green leaves have an odd number of smaller oval leaflets. The inedible fleshy green husk of the walnut encloses the nut, and the nut must be cracked to get the edible nutmeat.

Natural Range: Found throughout the Eastern United States, black walnut is found naturally growing from Vermont to Minnesota, south to Florida and Texas. It thrives in deep, well-drained soils. It is a shade-intolerant tree and must have direct sunlight to grow.

Food Usage: The primary food usage is the walnut. While the hard nut casing has antioxidants that help keep the nut oil from going rancid, the walnut must be stored properly to keep out insect and mold infestations. Because fungal mold creates aflatoxin, any mold in a walnut batch ruins the entire store. For home storage, the nuts should be kept in a low-humidity environment and between the temperatures of 27°F and 32°F. Once the nut is cracked open, the nutmeat can turn rancid within a week at room temperature, so it must be kept refrigerated, or better yet, frozen. Frozen, in vacuum-sealed bags, it will last for three years. Walnut meat may be candied, pickled, used raw, roasted, cooked, or baked in recipes, or turned into nut butter. I am fortunate in that I have several walnut trees near my house and get buckets of walnuts each year, so when researching which projects and recipes to use for this book, I was really able to try a lot of things for this particular tree. I could not narrow the food project down to one item so I decided to throw in a bonus recipe. We are going to show not only how to roast walnuts, but also cook them in pasta sauce.

Roasted Walnuts

Ingredients:
- Walnuts
- Nut oil (optional but preferred)
- Salt (optional)

Procedure:
1. Preheat oven to 350°F
2. Spread the nuts in an even layer on the baking sheet.
3. If you decide to use oil, use as little oil as possible. Drizzle a couple of teaspoons of oil over the nuts and toss to coat.
4. Place tray in oven and roast for 5 minutes.
5. Remove after 5 minutes and stir, return tray to oven.
6. Check the nuts again after 3 minutes. The nuts are done when the color is darker, they smell nutty, and you may hear them crackling. The process should take only 8 to 12 minutes.
7. Remove from the oven and immediately transfer onto a plate or another baking sheet to cool. They may scorch if you leave them in the hot tray.
8. Sprinkle salt on roasted nuts while they are hot.

A black walnut in its husk (top) and with husk removed (bottom). Credit: Mike Krebill.

Additional tips: Roasting nuts with a touch of oil is a really nice way to add flavor and crispness. Personally, I love oil-roasted nuts for snacking, but it does add oil, so be careful with this if you plan on using the nuts in a recipe. Close care must be taken as they can go from done to burnt in less than a minute. Smaller nuts cook faster than larger nuts so the preheating is critical to a good result. Chop the nuts after roasting them. Chopped nuts burn extremely easy and roasted nuts chop easier and with less flaking. I don't normally do this, but I have on occasion roasted nuts with honey as well.

A grove of English walnut trees in California.
English walnuts have thin, easily cracked shells.

Pasta with walnut sauce.

Pasta with Walnut Sauce

Ingredients:

- 1 slice bread, crusts removed
- 2/3 cup whole milk
- 6 ounces roasted walnuts, divided
- ½ clove garlic, minced
- 1 ounce grated Parmesan, plus more for garnish
- 3–4 tablespoons olive oil
- Salt and pepper
- 2 pounds any flat pasta broken into short lengths (tagliatelle, fettuccine, pappardelle, and linguine all work well)

Procedure:
1. Boil a large saucepan of water.
2. Put bread in a bowl and cover with milk.
3. Blend the toasted walnuts (reserve 1 ounce for later), garlic, bread soaked in milk, and Parmesan until the mix becomes smooth and creamy.
4. Pour the oil in the blender and season with salt and pepper and blend the mixture again.
5. Pour into a bowl, and set aside.
6. Add pasta to boiling water with salt and cook according to box directions until the pasta is al dente.
7. Reserving a cup of the pasta cooking liquid, drain the pasta and place in a large bowl while it is still dripping water.
8. Sprinkle some olive oil over the pasta to prevent it from sticking together.
9. Add walnut sauce, mixing it into the pasta (if the sauce is too thick, add a small amount of pasta water as needed).
10. Add remaining walnuts and Parmesan to pasta as a garnish.

Alternative Usage: Walnut stains everything. If you husk walnuts without gloves, you will probably have black-dyed hands a month. I have a friend who is a very experienced trapper (see the dedication to the book), and he has used walnuts to dye his snares and traps. Dried walnut husks have been used as ink. Leonardo da Vinci and Rembrandt used walnut ink for their work because it lasts so long. Walnuts were used as hair dye in ancient Rome and medieval Europe. When used with fabric, walnut makes a colorfast, wash- and light-resistant brown earth-toned dye that works great with natural fibers and makes an especially effective natural camouflage. The only real drawback is how effective it is at staining. If you choose not to wear gloves, you risk a very long-term recoloring of your hands, and you should keep the dye away from your good clothes.

Black Walnut Dye
Materials:
- 10–15 black walnuts
- Water
- 1 tablespoon washing soda
- ½ teaspoon detergent

Procedure:
1. This will make approximately 1 gallon of dye.
2. Remove the walnut husks.
3. Crush the hulls into pea-sized pieces.
4. Using a non-reactive pot (stainless steel or enamelware—*not* aluminum), bring 1 gallon water to a full boil.
5. Add the crushed hulls and stir.
6. Reduce heat and simmer, uncovered, for about an hour.

7. While the dye is simmering, scour the material you plan to dye. Scouring is the process of deeply cleaning the material so the dye can attach evenly. You can scour cotton by bringing water to a boil and simmering the cotton in a large nonreactive pot with a tablespoon of washing soda and a teaspoon of laundry detergent per gallon of water.

8. Using a non-reactive pot, add 1 tablespoon of washing soda and ½ teaspoon of detergent per 1 gallon of water and stir to dissolve.

9. Boil water.

10. Add the material you plan to dye and stir it into the water until it is fully saturated.

11. Reduce heat and simmer uncovered for 1 hour.

12. Rinse your materials to remove all the soap. Wring out the excess water.

13. Add the damp, scoured material to the simmering dye bath.

14. Continue to simmer, stirring occasionally, until the material is at least one shade darker than your desired color.

15. Remove the material and rinse thoroughly until the water runs clear.

16. Cool the dye bath and store in a glass container for reuse (do not pour out in your lawn or garden, as walnuts produce a natural herbicide).

17. Allow your materials to dry completely before using. The color will lighten some as it dries and the dye oxidizes.

Dyed clothing should be washed separately the first time. Excess dye will stain other clothes. After the initial wash, you may launder as usual with like-colored items.

Note: Don't compost walnut hulls, because they can suppress the growing of other plants. Tomatoes and apples, for example, won't grow near walnuts.

Walnut leaf.

Black walnut leaf.

Pine tree.

WHITE PINE

Scientific Name: *Pinus strobus*

Type of Plant: Evergreen tree

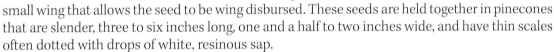

Pine leaves and cones
(Mike Krebill).

Description: The white pine is a large, straight-stemmed tree with long, horizontal branches that are upswept at the ends. The crown becomes irregular as the tree ages. It grows 50 to 180 feet tall. White pine leaves are four inches long, needle-shaped, and held in bundles of five. The needles are bluish green, straight, slender, and flexible. The leaf bundles live for 18 months before they are shed and replaced by a new needle bundle. The seeds are less than ⅛ inch long and have a small wing that allows the seed to be wing disbursed. These seeds are held together in pinecones that are slender, three to six inches long, one and a half to two inches wide, and have thin scales often dotted with drops of white, resinous sap.

Natural Range: White pine grows from Canada south to Northern Georgia and Northeastern Alabama and west to Minnesota. It prefers limestone soil with good drainage and mild summers. It has commercial use as lumber, so it may be planted outside its normal habitat.

Food Usage: Pine trees have many edible parts. The young needle shoots can be eaten, the bark can be boiled and ground to use as a famine food replacement for flour, but the best edible use of pine is to steep the needles for a tea that is high in vitamins A and C.

Pine Needle Tea

Ingredients:
- Small handful of young needles
- Water

Procedure:
1. Remove any of the brown, papery sheaths that may remain at the base of the needles.
2. Chop the needles into small ¼- to ½-inch-long pieces.
3. Heat about a cup of water to just before boiling.
4. Pour the hot water over about a tablespoon of the chopped needles.
5. Cover and allow to steep for 5–10 minutes.

Alternative Usage: Pine secretes a resin to close cuts or broken limbs. This sticky sap has several uses during survival situations. As pine sap is exposed to air, it will harden, but heating can soften it. The pine resin is waterproof, so it can be heated and applied to materials to seal seams or used as glue. It is flammable and can be used to help start fires. Fatwood that survivalists prize as a fire starter is simply aged pine stumps that have the resin concentrated in the wood.

Pine Pitch Glue

Materials:
- Pine pitch
- Charcoal
- Stick with a blunt end

Procedure:

1. Warm the resin to liquid form (a double boiler is best, as pine pitch is very flammable).
2. Crumble charcoal as fine as possible.
3. Once the resin is liquid, remove it from the heat.
4. Stir in powdered charcoal. The ratio of charcoal to liquid pine sap should be one to three.
5. Dip the stick in the liquid pine/charcoal mix. Do this repeatedly to form a large clump of pitch on the end of the stick. Once the glue hardens, the stick is easily stored for use.

Pine resin.

To Use: Heat until pliable and rub over material to be joined. Additionally, the pitch on the end of the stick may be lighted and used as a torch.

Notes: Pine tar mixed with sulfur is useful to treat dandruff. Pine sap can be chewed like gum to clean your teeth. Pine tar can also be processed to make turpentine.

White pine needle cluster
(Mike Krebill).

WILLOW

Weeping willow tree.

Scientific Name: *Salix babylonica*
Type of Plant: Deciduous tree
Description: Willows grow between 35 and 50 feet tall and develop a crown of the same size but have an extremely developed root system that is often larger than the tree. Willow roots have been known to destroy septic systems and sidewalks in developed areas. The wood is soft, usually pliant, and tough. The slender branches are filled with a watery bark sap that is heavily concentrated with salicylic acid. The leaves are typically elongated, simple, and feather-veined.
Natural Range: Willows can be found throughout the United States, with weeping willows found primarily on the coasts. Because of their ability to absorb large amounts of water, they are often planted in flood zones or areas that need to be drained. The strong root system also prevents erosion.

Food Usage: Willow is edible, but it is unappetizing and is best considered to be a famine food. The inner bark is edible, but first needs to be boiled several times to remove the bitterness caused by the salicylic acid. In Scandinavia, the boiled inner bark is dried, pulverized into dust, and added to flour to extend it. Historically, sawdust of all types has been used during famines as a flour extender. I prefer to utilize willow saplings to make frog gigs. Since the edible parts of the tree are so bitter and it grows next to water, it makes sense to skip the bark and go for the meat.

Willow Sapling Frog Gig

Materials:

- Straight willow sapling 6–8 feet long and about 2 inches in diameter
- Green twig 3 inches long (about the size of your little finger)
- Cordage

Procedure:

Frog gig from survivalsherpa.wordpress.com/tag/how-to-make-a-frog-gig.

1. Trim the sapling of all limbs.
2. Strip the bark off the smaller end of the stick, clearing a spot about 1 foot long.
3. Place the root end of the sapling (the larger of the two ends) on a large rock or stump.
4. Use a knife to split the thin end of the shaft 7 or 8 inches deep.
5. Turn the sapling 90 degrees and make a second split to the same depth perpendicular to the first, making 4 equal pieces
6. Split the 3-inch twig into 2 halves.
7. Wedge the first half into a split in the shaft to use as a spreader.
8. Install the other spreader into the opposite split.
9. Sharpen the 4 spread tines to turn them into sharpened points. You may add barbs, but the tines are spread enough so that barbs are both unnecessary and weakening of the points.

Willow leaf.

10. Lash the spreaders to the shaft.
11. Trim the spreaders flush with the lashings.

Keep in mind that when using the gig, light is refracted, making the object of attention look behind where it actually is, and so aim low.

Alternative Usage: While the willow is not the greatest wild edible, it has outstanding alternative uses, of which I am going to share two. Willow trees make an excellent rooting hormone that allows almost any cutting to be rooted. Willow roots so easily that the new growth can root itself, similar to strawberries or blackberries. My dad recently cut some willow, and the cut logs sent up shoots to root.

The second alternative use is extracting salicylic acid, which is the natural version of aspirin. However, note that salicylic acid is rough on your stomach, which means you should not take more than a cup or two of willow tea without both understanding your body and seeking the advice of your doctor.

Willow Rooting Hormone

Materials:
- First year willow twigs with green or yellow bark
- Water

Procedure:
1. Cut the twigs into 1-inch pieces.
2. Place the chopped willow twigs in a container.
3. Cover the twigs with boiling water.
4. Let steep overnight.
5. Separate the liquid from the twigs by carefully pouring the liquid through a strainer.
6. To use, pour some willow water into a small jar, and place cuttings in the jar as you would put flowers in a vase.
7. Let soak overnight.
8. Remove from water and plant as you would any cutting.

You can keep the liquid for up to two months if you put it in a sealed jar in the refrigerator.

Rooting hormone in use.

Growing Willows for Baskets and Other Uses

Because they are so easily propagated by cuttings, you can grow a willow tree by simply pushing a small fresh willow twig a few inches into the soil in late winter to early spring. I have done this to make living fences that a person can shape and mold as desired.

Willow trees are also traditionally grown for baskets, but unlike willows that are planted and shaped for fences, willows grown for basket making are often coppiced.

Coppicing is a method of managing trees using the ability of willow (and some other trees) to grow new shoots from their stump if the tree is cut down. An adult willow is cut down, and as new flexible stems emerge, they are cut down at ground level to be used as material for weaving. This can be done repeatedly over decades.

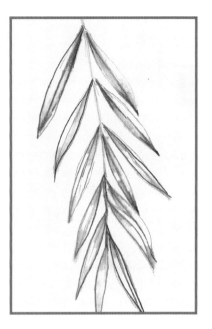

Willow leaf.

Willow tree.

7

PLANTS AND SHRUBS

This section contains 25 common and easily identified smaller plants. Some can be found growing in cracks in city sidewalks or suburban yards. Almost all of the following plants grow throughout the United States.

As with all adventure activities, be sure you are safe and that you fully identify plants before you attempt to eat them.

Dandelion. Courtesy of kikiricky (CC SA 3.0).

AMARANTH

Growing amaranth.

Scientific Name: *Amaranthus*

Type of Plant: Annual (sometimes, though rarely, perennial)

Description: Amaranth is characterized by small, often green or reddish flowers arranged in dense clusters, stems, and leaves that are dry, deeply pigmented, indehiscent, and have a one-seeded fruit.

There are about 70 species in this genus of herbaceous plants. Amaranth is sometimes called pigweed.

Although several species are often considered invasive weeds, people around the world value amaranths as leaf vegetables, cereals, and ornamentals.

Natural Range: Amaranth grows worldwide, is very hardy, and requires little water to grow.

Food Usage: Amaranth seeds can be used as a cereal or ground into flour. The seeds are a great source of protein and are exceptionally complete for a plant protein source. Besides protein, amaranth grains are also a good source of dietary fiber and dietary minerals such as iron, magnesium, phosphorus, copper, and especially manganese. However, amaranth is not a true grain, because the plant is not in the grass family. Like quinoa, it is a "pseudograin" because the flavor, appearance, and cooked forms of many species exhibit similarities to grain. The leaves also are consumed as a nutritious leaf vegetable, being used both in cooking and salads.

Amaranth flower.

Raw amaranth grain.

Cooked Amaranth Grain

Ingredients:
- One cup of amaranth seeds
- 2½–3 cups water

Procedure:
1. Combine amaranth seeds with 2½ cups water in a pot and bring to a boil.
2. Reduce heat, cover, and simmer for up to 20 minutes, until grains are fluffy and water is absorbed.
3. For a porridge-like consistency, use slightly more water (3 cups for 1 cup grain) and cook a little longer.

Amaranth leaves.

Alternative Usage: This takes some practice, but you can pop (puff) amaranth like popcorn. Be aware you are probably going to burn it the first few times, since it is tricky to make.

Popped Amaranth Grains

Materials:

- 1 cup amaranth grain
- Wok or skillet
- Fine mesh metal strainer

Procedure:

1. Start with a dry skillet or pan and heat it to high.
2. Spoon 1 teaspoon amaranth grains into your pan once the pan is good and hot.
3. Don't be discouraged if the grains don't pop right away or if they burn. If grains are burning, the pan isn't hot enough. They should start popping within a couple seconds of entering the pan.
4. Continue until all grain has been popped.
5. Store popped amaranth in an airtight glass container in your fridge or pantry for 4–6 weeks.

Notes: Red dye and oil can also be made from the seeds.

Amaranth flower.

Puffed amaranth grain.

BLACKBERRIES

Scientific Name: *Rubus allegheniensis*
Type of Plant: Bramble
Description: The *bramble*, a word meaning any impenetrable thicket, has traditionally been applied specifically to the blackberry or its products. They are the largest of all berries. They are plump and have a purple-black color. In reality, blackberries are not berries at all; they are tiny fruits clustered together around a core. Each tiny fruit contains a little seed. The plant has white flowers and its leaves typically feature five leaflets.

Blackberryleaf and flower. Courtesy of Nicholas A Tonelli (CC BY 2.0).

Natural Range: Blackberries grow throughout the United States, Europe, and Asia.
Food Usage: The berries have been enjoyed naturally or cooked by multiple cultures throughout the ages.

Blackberry Sauce

Ingredients:
- 3½ cups fresh blackberries
- ¼ cup sugar or honey
- ¼ cup water
- 1 tablespoon lemon juice

Procedure:
1. Bring blackberries, sugar, and water to a simmer in a medium saucepan, stirring occasionally.
2. Simmer over low heat for 5 minutes.
3. Strain through a fine sieve into a bowl.
4. Stir in lemon juice.
5. Cover and refrigerate until chilled.

Blackberry sauce over ice cream.

Blackberry leaves.

Blackberry fruit.

Blackberry bramble.

Alternative Usage: Blackberry leaf tea was used by the colonists of New England when tea was first expensive to import and later difficult to get after the Boston Tea Party.

Blackberry Tea

Ingredients:
- 2 tablespoons dried blackberry leaves
- 1½ cups water

Procedure:
1. Steep dried blackberry leaves in water for 10 minutes.
2. Strain.

Notes: Blackberries are perennial plants that typically bear biennial stems from their root system.

BROADLEAF PLANTAIN

Scientific Name: *Plantago major*
Type of Plant: Perennial
Description: Broadleaf plantain is a perennial herb that grows from a rosette of leaves that is six to twelve inches in diameter. Each oval-shaped leaf is two to eight inches long and one and a half to four inches wide. The flowers are small, brown with a purplish tint, and have purple stamens that are produced in a dense spike two to six inches long on top of a stem five to six inches tall.
Natural Range: Broadleaf plantain is native to most of Europe and Northern and Central Asia, but it has spread widely throughout the world.
Food Usage: Broadleaf plantain is a very nutritious wild food. It has large amounts of calcium and vitamins A, C, and K. The leaves are edible as a salad green when young and tender, but they quickly become tough, bitter, and fibrous as they get older. However, older leaves can be stewed to tenderize them.

Pan-fried Plantain and Onions

Ingredients:
- 2 tablespoons olive oil, divided
- 1 medium onion, diced
- 2 bell peppers, sliced
- 3 cups fresh plantain leaves
- 2 tablespoons apple cider vinegar
- Salt and pepper

Procedure:
1. Pour 1 tablespoon olive oil into pan and heat to medium high.
2. Add onion and pepper and cook until onion is translucent.
3. Add the plantain and the rest of the oil.

Plantain leaf and flower spike.

4. Cook until you get the desired tenderness. Too much heat will cause the leaves to disintegrate—I feel that 3–5 minutes is best.
5. Finish with the apple cider vinegar and a pinch of salt and pepper.

Roasted Plantain Chips

Ingredients:
- 2 cups young common plantain leaves
- 2 teaspoons sesame oil
- ½ teaspoon ground fennel seeds
- ½ teaspoon caraway seeds
- ¼ teaspoon powdered ginger
- ½ teaspoon salt
- Hot sauce

Plantain plant.

Plantain leaf.

Procedure:
1. Preheat oven to 425°F.
2. Mix all the ingredients together until the leaves are evenly coated. Spread onto oiled cookie sheets. I normally use parchment paper or nonstick silicone mats instead of oil.
3. Bake about 6 minutes, stirring occasionally, until very lightly browned and crisp. Be careful not to let the leaves burn.

Note: This recipe is the same for making kale chips, and I find that everything but the leaves, salt, and oil are optional.

Narrowleaf plantain.

Burdock plant.

Burdock leaf.

BURDOCK

Scientific Name: *Arctium lappa*
Type of Plant: Biennial
Description: Greater burdock tall plant growing to 10 feet tall. Burdock has dark green leaves that can grow up to 28 inches long. The leaves are generally large, coarse, and ovate, with the lower ones being heart-shaped. They are woolly underneath.
Natural Range: Burdock is native to Europe and Asia, but it has been widely introduced worldwide.
Food Usage: The burdock roots can be eaten as a root vegetable, and it can substitute for carrot in recipes.

Pickled Burdock Root

Ingredients:
- 8 oz. peeled burdock root, sliced into ¼-inch coins
- 2 cups water
- 1 teaspoon kosher salt
- ¼ cup white vinegar
- Favorite pickling herbs

Procedure:
1. Place the sliced and peeled burdock in a pot with the water and salt.
2. Bring the mixture to a boil, turn down heat, cover, and simmer for 15–20 minutes. You want the burdock to soften to the texture of a cooked artichoke, soft and yielding but still slightly firm.
3. Add the vinegar and spices to the burdock when it is cooked through.
4. Process in a water bath canner in a pint jar for 15 minutes.

Greater burdock plant.

Candied Burdock

Ingredients:
- Immature burdock flower stalk
- Pinch of baking soda
- 1 cup sugar
- ½ cup water
- 1 lemon, zested and juiced
- Granulated sugar

Procedure:
1. Remove the green rind. Slice the stalk into the desired final shape.
2. Boil in water with a pinch of baking soda for 20 minutes.
3. Drain.
4. Simmer the slices until clear in a syrup made from 1 cup sugar, ½ cup water, and the juice and grated zest of a lemon.
5. Drain.
6. Roll in granulated sugar just before serving.

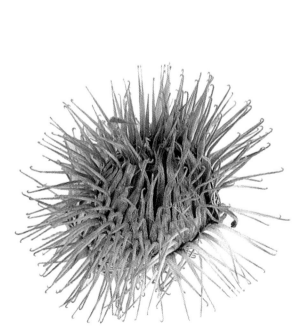

Notes: Velcro was invented after an inventor noticed the burdock seed pods attached to his dog's fur.

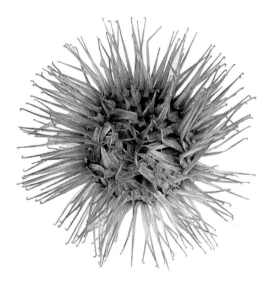

Burdock burr.

CATTAILS

Marsh featuring *Typha angustifolia*

Scientific Name: *Typha latifolia* (broadleaf cattail) and *Typha angustifolia* (narrowleaf cattail)
Type of Plant: Perennial
Description: Cattail leaves are on a simple, jointless stem that bears the flowering spikes. The flowers form a narrow spike at the top of the vertical stem. The seeds are minute and attached to fine hairs. When ripe, the heads disintegrate into a cottony fluff from which the seeds disperse by wind.
Natural Range: Cattails are found in wetland habitats throughout the Northern Hemisphere.

Cattail rush.

Food Usage: Many parts of the plant are edible by humans. The starchy rhizomes are nutritious with protein content comparable to corn or rice. They are most often harvested from late autumn to early spring. The outer portion of young plants can be peeled and the heart can be eaten raw or boiled and eaten like asparagus.

Cattail on the Cob

Ingredients:
- 30–40 cattail flower heads, peeled
- Water
- Butter

Procedure:
1. Boil cattail flower heads in water for 10 minutes.
2. Drain the cattail flower heads and slather them generously with butter.
3. Eat them just like miniature corn on the cob.

Leaves and cattail head of *Typha latifolia*.

Alternative Usage: Some Native American Indians used the seed hairs as tinder for starting fires. Some tribes also used cattail down to line moccasins and for bedding, diapers, baby powder, and cradleboards.

Cattails can be dipped in wax or fat and then lit as a candle, the stem serving as a wick. Without the use of wax or fat it will smolder slowly, somewhat like incense, and may repel insects.

Cattail Candle

Materials:
- Dry cattail flower heads
- Rendered lard, wax, or oil
- Stick with sharpened end

Procedure:
1. Dip the cattail head into a container filled with melted lard, wax, or oil. The higher quality of fuel you use, the better your candle will perform.
2. Remove the cattail and let the melted fat harden.
3. Insert the stick into the head.
4. Light the cattail. This candle is more of a torch and can burn upwards of 6 hours, producing plenty of light and heat.

Cattail flower spike.

Note: No green plant produces more edible starch per acre than cattails. In addition, cattails can be used to produce shelter, fire, baskets, and much more.

CHICKWEED

Chickweed flower up close.

Scientific Name: *Stellaria media*
Type of Plant: Annual
Description: Chickweed grows to 15 inches tall on weak slender stems. It is sparsely hairy, with hairs in a line along the stem. The leaves are oval and opposite, the lower ones with stalks. Flowers are white and small with five very deeply lobed petals. Flowers are followed quickly by the seed pods. This plant flowers and sets seed at the same time.
Natural Range: Native to Europe, chickweed has been naturalized throughout North America. It is very common in lawns, open areas, along trails, and in waste areas.

Chickweed.

Food Usage: Chickweed can be useful as livestock forage (but in huge quantities it can be toxic to cattle). Humans often eat it raw in salads as a leaf vegetable, and it can be treated like a leafy green in other recipes.

Chickweed Bread

Ingredients:

- ¼ cup minced onion
- 2 cups chopped chickweed leaves and stems.
- 2 tablespoons oil
- 2 tablespoons honey, fruit juice concentrate, or sugar
- 1 packet yeast
- ¾ cup warm water
- 1 teaspoon salt
- 3 cups wheat flour

Chickweed leaves.

Procedure:

1. Sauté onion and chickweed in oil until tender (but NOT caramelized).
2. Dissolve honey and yeast into warm water
3. Add salt to yeast mix.
4. Mix the yeast mixture with the cooled sautéed chickweed and onions.
5. Slowly add the flour until the dough no longer sticks to your fingers.
6. Form into a ball and let it rise to twice its volume.
7. Shape into loaves and let rise again.
8. Bake at 375°F for 40–45 minutes.

Chickweed Pesto

Ingredients:

- 2–4 cloves garlic, minced
- ½ cup extra virgin olive oil
- 2–3 cups freshly picked young chickweed leaves
- ¼ cup freshly grated parmesan cheese
- Dash of sea salt
- Handful of walnuts (optional)
- 1 tablespoon lemon juice (optional)
- Lemon zest (optional)

Procedure:

1. Place all the ingredients in a food processor. Blend well.
2. You can use fresh or freeze in ice cube trays for later use.

Serving Suggestions:
Chickweed pesto makes a great sandwich spread; it also tastes good spooned on eggs, meat, or vegetables. It is tradionally used as a pasta sauce and is sometimes spread over boiled potatoes or raw tomato slices.

Buttered Chickweed
Ingredients:
- 2 cups chickweed, thoroughly washed and chopped
- 1 onion, finely chopped
- 1 tablespoon butter (more if desired)
- Salt
- Pepper

Procedure:
1. Place chickweed in boiling salted water. Cook for only 2–3 minutes. Drain well. (Save the water as it makes an excellent liquid for cooking rice.)
2. Melt butter in a frying pan. Sauté the onion until translucent.
3. Add chickweed and salt and pepper to taste. Sauté 1 minute to finish.

Notes: Chickweed is often called common chickweed to distinguish it from other plants called chickweed. Other common names include chickenwort, craches, maruns, and winterweed. Chickweed can form large mats of foliage.

Chickweed flower.

A close-up of the chickweed's single row of hairs (Mike Krebill).

CLOVER (RED AND WHITE)

Red clover.

Scientific Name: *Trifolium repens* (white clover), *Trifolium pratense* (red clover)
Type of Plant: Perennial
Description: Clovers typically have three leaflets per leaf. White clover's flower has its own stalk, separate from the leaf. Red clover flowers and leaves are on the same branching stalk. Both have a lighter colored chevron or V-pattern on their leaflets, which helps to distinguish them from other plants with three leaflets per leaf when the flowers aren't present. White clover is a short perennial, often found in lawns. It grows three to nine inches tall. Red clover is taller, growing to 7 to 28 inches. It is more often grown as either forage or as a cover crop.
Natural Range: Native to Europe, Western Asia, and Northwest Africa, it also has been naturalized in other continents, including North and South America.

White clover.

Food Usage: While not often thought of as an edible plant, all of the aerial parts of the clover plant are edible: leaves, stems, flowers, and seedpods. The dried leaves and flowers are slightly sweet and can leave behind a faint vanilla-like flavor. Use them fresh or dried in baked goods. Use the leaves raw in salads or dry for baked goods later. The flowers make a delicious tea and can be used dried or fresh.

White Clover Pudding

Ingredients:
- 1 tablespoon unflavored gelatin
- 1¼ cup water, divided
- 2 cups white clover blossoms
- ½ cup fresh squeezed orange juice
- 4 tablespoons honey
- Pinch of salt
- 1 cup heavy cream (or 1 cup full-fat Greek yogurt)

Procedure:
1. Dissolve gelatin in ¼ cup water.
2. Slowly bring to a boil the white clover blossoms, 1 cup water, orange juice, honey, and salt.
3. Remove from heat, and stir in gelatin until completely dissolved. Allow to stand for 10 minutes.
4. Place covered in refrigerator until the mixture begins to gel.
5. While mixture cools, whip heavy cream (if using) until it stiffens.
6. Fold whipped cream (or yogurt) into the gelled clover mixture.
7. Place in a serving bowl and refrigerate until set.

White Clover Iced Tea

Ingredients:
- 1 cup fresh white clover blossoms or ½ cup dried blossoms
- 4 cups water
- Honey or maple syrup (optional)
- Lemon (optional)

Procedure:
1. Boil water. Put the clover blossoms into a quart jar.
2. Pour boiling water over the blossoms. Let steep for at least 30 minutes, or up to 4 hours.
3. Strain out the clover blossoms with a fine mesh sieve and refrigerate.
4. Serve cold over ice with honey or maple syrup and lemon if desired.

Sautéed Clover

Ingredients:
- ½ pound clover
- 3 tablespoons vegetable oil
- ½ teaspoon salt
- ½ teaspoon soy sauce

Procedure:
1. Wash the clover well, ensuring you remove any weeds or grass. Drain in a colander, and shake thoroughly. (The clover will release a lot of liquid while cooking.)
2. Heat the oil in skillet (or preferably a wok) until it just starts to smoke.
3. Add clover and stir-fry with a scooping motion for 10 seconds, ensuring that the clover does not get burned.
4. Add the salt and soy sauce, and continue to stir until the seasonings are mixed in and the entire clover becomes wilted, about 15 seconds more. Remove from heat and serve immediately.

Clover leaves.

Clover flower.

Strawberry White Clover Cookies

Ingredients:

- 3 cups all-purpose flour
- 1 teaspoon baking soda
- 1 cup butter, softened
- ¾ cup packed brown sugar
- 2 eggs
- 2 tablespoons milk
- ½ cup packed (⅜ oz.) fresh white clover blossoms, chopped
- 1 cup (5 oz.) strawberries, diced

Procedure:

1. Preheat oven to 350°F. Line cookie sheets with parchment paper or silicone baking mats.
2. Sift together the flour and baking soda. Set aside.
3. Cream together the butter and brown sugar until light and fluffy. Add the eggs and beat well. Stir in the milk.
4. Beat the dry ingredients into the batter until well combined.
5. Fold in the clover blossoms and strawberries and mix until combined.
6. Drop dough (about 1 tablespoon) onto prepared baking sheets.
7. Bake in preheated oven for 13–15 minutes. Edges will be golden brown.
8. Cool on wire cooling racks.

Notes: The shamrock, the traditional Irish symbol that (according to legend) was coined by Saint Patrick for the Holy Trinity, is commonly associated with clover.

Clovers occasionally have four leaflets, instead of the usual three. These four-leaf clovers, like other rarities, are considered lucky. Clovers can also have five, six, or more leaflets, but these are rarer. The record for most leaflets is 56, set in 2009 in Japan.

COMFREY

Common comfrey plant.

Scientific Name: *Symphytum officinale*
Type of Plant: Perennial
Description: Comfrey is a perennial herb with a black, turnip-like root and large, broad, hairy leaves. Comfrey bears small bell-shaped flowers of various colors (but most often purple or cream). These flowers can also appear to be striped. It likes to grow in damp, grassy places, and is often found on riverbanks and ditches. Because it is tolerant of many different soil conditions and can sew itself, comfrey can spread rapidly.
Natural Range: Comfrey is hardy and grows across the United States. It will grow in full or partial sun.

Comfrey
flowers.

Food Usage: Comfrey leaves have a hairy and rough texture as they age, making them unappetizing to eat if too old. However, because it is a good source of magnesium and selenium, as well as being very high in vitamin A, riboflavin, potassium, manganese, and dietary fiber, comfrey is worth the trouble. Young comfrey leaves and buds are very tender.

Comfrey Soap

Ingredients:
- 1 pound pure lard (also known as manteca)
- 3 oz. lye (sodium hydroxide)
- 1 oz. distilled water (not tap, filtered, or bottled mineral)
- 1 teaspoon dried calendula petals
- 1 teaspoon dried chamomile flowers
- 1 teaspoon dried ground comfrey root or leaves

Procedure:
1. Prepare your mold.
2. Weigh out and place lard into a large pot.
3. Prepare the lye solution by measuring out the water and the sodium hydroxide. Slowly pour the sodium hydroxide into the water and gently stir until the crystals dissolve. It will get hot. (*Always* add lye to water for safety reasons.)
4. Once the lye solution has become clear, slowly pour the lye water over the hard lard in your pot. The hot solution will melt the lard. Gently press the lard down into the lye solution with the whisk and slowly stir until the lard is completely melted.
5. Using an immersion blender, mix the soap batter in short bursts, alternating with hand stirring until the soap starts to thicken like a pudding.
6. When thickened, add dried calendula petals, dried chamomile flowers, and dried ground comfrey root or leaves. Stir well to incorporate.
7. Pour into the prepared soap mold. Wrap and insulate until the soap sets.
8. As soon as the soap has cooled to the touch and is firm enough to handle, you can cut it into bars. Cure the soap for 4 to 6 weeks. This makes the soap milder and less harsh on your skin.

Comfrey plant.

Comfrey flower.

Note: All of the plant material must be dried or it can cause soap to spoil.

A liquid fertilizer can also be made from the comfrey plant by steeping chopped comfrey leaves in water for several weeks until they form a dark, thick liquid. The liquid should be diluted 12:1 before application.

A potting mixture can also be made from leaf mold derived from chopped comfrey leaves and dolomite mixed together and left to sit in a lidded container for several months. Though not suitable for seeds, once well-rotted, the comfrey leaf mixture is a good general potting soil.

Comfrey salve.

COMMON EVENING PRIMROSE

Scientific Name: *Oenothera biennis*
Type of Plant: Biennial
Description: *Oenothera biennis* has a life span of two years. The plant grows to 12 to 59 inches tall. The leaves are shaped like spear tips, about two to eight inches long and a half inch to one inch broad, and they are produced in a tight rosette the first year but spirally on a stem the second year.

Primroses bloom from late spring to late summer. The flowers are hermaphroditic, produced on a tall spike, and only last until the following noon. They open visibly quickly every evening, which is the origin of the name "evening primrose."

The yellow blooms, one to two inches in diameter, have four bilobed petals. The flowers feature a bright nectar guiding pattern that is invisible to the naked eye but apparent under ultraviolet light and visible to moths, butterflies, and bees.

Natural Range: Common evening primrose is native to Eastern and Central North America, from Canada to Texas and Florida. It is widely naturalized throughout the world in temperate and subtropical regions.

Food Usage: Virtually all parts of the common evening primrose are edible. It normally has a mild taste, but occasionally it has what is described as a rough aftertaste. The roots of a young plant (from about September until the first flowering stem is developed) can be eaten raw or cooked like potatoes. The leaves can be eaten raw or cooked from April to June when the plant is not yet flowering. The flowering stems are best harvested in June; once peeled, they can be eaten raw or fried. The flower buds are a delicacy and can be harvested from June to September. They are eaten raw in salads, pickled in oil, fried, or in soups. The sweet-tasting flowers are edible as well; they can be used as garnish for salads but also in desserts. When the fruits are still green in August and September, they can be used similar to the flowering stems.

Common evening primrose.

Close-up of flower and leaf of common
evening primrose.

Evening Primrose Leaf Burgers

Ingredients:
- 4½ cups chopped young evening primrose leaves
- 4½ cups barley or whole-wheat flour
- 4 cups coarsely chopped, cooked, and mashed carrots
- 4 cups chopped onions
- 3 cups cooked brown rice
- 3 cups water
- 2 cups fruit juice
- 2 cups roasted sesame seeds
- 3–5 tablespoons paprika
- 3 tablespoons miso paste
- 2 tablespoons fresh dill (or 2 teaspoons dried dill)
- 1 tablespoon oregano
- 1 teaspoon sea salt, or to taste
- ½ cup sesame oil

Procedure:
1. Mix all the ingredients together. You may need to add a little more barley or flour to get the right consistency; feel free to experiment.

Common evening primroses.

2. Shape into burgers.
3. Fry in sesame oil.

Pickled Evening Primrose Roots

This pickled primrose root recipe is great as a condiment or to add to salads and stir fry recipes. You can use the leftover vinegar to make salad dressings, cook greens, marinate meats, and any other use of vinegar you can think of.

Ingredients:
  • Pint jar of primrose root
  • 3 cups of raw apple cider vinegar
  • Rosemary (one teaspoon per cup of vinegar)
  • Garlic cloves (to taste)
  • Tablespoon of raw honey (to taste)
Procedure:
  1. Wash and roughly chop your roots.
  2. Put them in a glass jar.
  3. Cover with raw apple cider vinegar.
  4. Add rosemary, garlic, and honey to taste.
  5. Let sit for at least 2 weeks, or longer.

Note: During World War II, the seeds of the evening primrose were roasted and used as a coffee substitute.

COMMON MILKWEED

Milkweed flowers and leaves.

Milkweed leaf.

Scientific Name: *Asclepias syriaca*

Type of Plant: Perennial

Description: Milkweed grows up to six feet tall. It has large, broad leaves, usually four to ten inches long. The leaves sometimes have red veins. When the pods are crushed, they release a milky sap that the milkweed is named for.

Natural Range: This plant is found in fields, gardens, and along roads throughout the United States (except for the Pacific Northwest).

Food Usage: The boiled young shoots, leaves, unopened flower buds, flowers, and young pods are edible and most often consumed as cooked greens, cooked vegetables, or fritters. While common milkweed (*Asclepias syriaca*) is edible, not all milkweed species are. Some, like butterfly weed, swamp milkweed, and whorled milkweed, are considered poisonous.

Milkweed flowers.

Milkweed silk from seedpod.

Sautéed Milkweed Pods

Ingredients:
- Two dozen small, whole milkweed pods, each shorter than 2 inches in length
- 1 to 1½ cups all-purpose flour
- 2 tablespoons unsalted butter
- 1 tablespoon olive oil
- Salt and pepper

Procedure:
1. Place pods in a 4-quart saucepan and cover with cold water.
2. Bring to a boil, and boil pods for 10 minutes.
3. Place one cup of flour in a plastic bag. Place 6 pods in the bag and shake to coat with flour. Spread coated pods on a towel. Repeat until all of the pods are coated.
4. In a large skillet, melt the butter in the oil.
5. Add pods and allow them to cook without stirring for 3–4 minutes until the undersides form a golden crust.
6. Stir and cook another 3–5 minutes until the pods are tender.
7. Season with salt and pepper.

Alternative Usage: The fine milkweed fibers are great for making cordage.

Milkweed String

Material:
- Milkweed plant

Procedure:
1. Harvest the plant and let it dry.
2. Break up the stalk and pull long pieces off and set them aside.
3. "Thigh-roll" the pieces to make cord. Use two small bunches of fibers that are of different length. Hold the ends of two in your left hand. Drape their other ends over your right thigh. Roll the strands down your thigh using the palm and thumb of your right hand so that the strands "S" twist up. At the end of the roll, release the hold of your left hand on the fibers and allow the strands to "Z" twist in the opposite direction.
4. To make even string, continually splice new strands of fiber every couple of inches.
5. To splice in a length of fiber, lay the new piece along the shorter of the two original strands.
6. Twist the new and original fiber together as one strand and continue rolling the cordage. Each time a new piece is spliced in, leave an inch or so of the new fiber projecting from the plied cord; these can be trimmed off when the cord is finished.

Milkweed pod.

Notes: The milkweed filaments are hollow and coated with wax, and have good insulation qualities. During World War II, over five thousand tons of milkweed floss was collected in the United States as a substitute for the original kapok filling in flotation vests. Milkweed is grown commercially as a hypoallergenic filling for pillows. Milkweed is also beneficial to nearby plants, repelling some pests, especially wireworms.

COMMON YARROW

Young yarrow plants.

Scientific Name: *Achillea millefolium*
Type of Plant: Perennial
Description: Common yarrow is an erect, herbaceous, perennial plant that produces one to several stems approximately 16 inches tall. Leaves are evenly distributed along the stem, with the leaves near the middle and bottom of the stem being the largest. The leaves have varying degrees of hair. The leaves are two to eight inches long, feathery, and arranged spirally on the stems. The plant has a strong, sweet scent, similar to that of chrysanthemums.
Natural Range: Common yarrow prefers sunny locations on thin, sandy soils, although it can grow in partial sun conditions as well. Yarrow is commonly found along roadsides, in fields, waste areas, canyon bottoms, and even on lawns. It grows in North America, Europe, Asia, Australia, Africa, and South America.

Yarrow flower.

Food Usage: Leaves can be consumed raw or cooked. They have a somewhat bitter flavor, yet they make a great addition to mixed salads. They are best used when young.

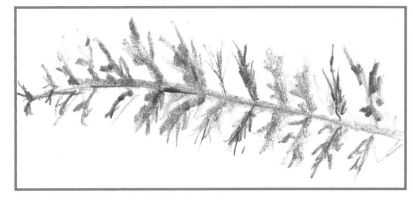
Yarrow leaf.

Yarrow Pasta

Ingredients:
- A large handful of yarrow leaves picked from the stem and chopped
- 1 teaspoon crushed red pepper
- Pinch of kosher salt
- 8 ounces dried penne pasta
- 4 tablespoons fresh garlic, finely chopped
- 3 tablespoons extra virgin olive oil
- 3 tablespoons canola oil
- 4 anchovy filets in oil, rinsed and chopped
- ¼ cup dry white wine (optional)
- Parmesan cheese

Procedure:
1. Mince the yarrow and crushed red pepper.
2. Bring a large pot of water to boil and add salt.
3. Cook pasta in water until it offers a slight resistance when bitten into, but is not soft (al dente).
4. While the pasta is cooking, heat the garlic in the pan with oil and anchovy filets on low heat until the garlic is fragrant and lightly browned.
5. If desired, add the wine to the pan.
6. Drain pasta and add to the pan.
7. Toss the pasta to coat with the oil and cook for a minute to evaporate any raw wine flavor.
8. Add the yarrow mixture and toss just to heat through.
9. Garnish with parmesan cheese.

Alternative Usage: Common yarrow has historical use in traditional medicine, and has been used as a diaphoretic, astringent, tonic, stimulant, and mild aromatic. The most common use is to stop bleeding and assist in wound healing. Put dry or fresh yarrow leaf on a bleeding wound, and hold pressure. It will usually stop the bleeding within 10 to 30 seconds.

Yarrow Salad

Ingredients:
- 3.5 oz. yarrow leaves
- 2 oz. breadcrumbs
- 1 egg
- 4 tablespoons balsamic vinegar
- ½ cup olive oil
- Salt to taste
- Pinch of sugar

Procedure:
1. Rinse the yarrow. Trim and rip into small pieces as needed. Drain well and transfer to plates.
2. Mix breadcrumbs with the egg and stir-fry in a pan with 3–4 tablespoons olive oil until crumbly and golden brown. Drain on paper towels and sprinkle with salt to taste.
3. Mix the vinegar with 3–4 tablespoons olive oil and season with salt and sugar. Drizzle over the yarrow and serve sprinkled with the breadcrumbs.

Yarrow flowers.

DANDELION

Dandelion seed head.

Scientific Name: *Taraxacum officinale*
Type of Plant: Perennial
Description: Like other members of the Asteraceae family, dandelions have very small flowers situated together into a composite flower head. Dandelions are tap-rooted herbs. The flower heads are yellow to orange colored, are open in the daytime, and closed at night.

Dandelion is one of my favorite plants. It is everywhere, and it's pretty useful. Dandelions can be used to make products as varied as dandelion syrup and coffee substitute.
Natural Range: Dandelions are found on all continents with the exception of Anarctica, and they are a commonly found plant in yards and open areas in temperate regions.

Young dandelion.

Sautéed dandelion.

Food Usage: Roots and leaves have been gathered for food since prehistory, but they are bitter. They are often blanched to remove bitterness or sautéed in the same way as spinach. Dandelion leaves contain several vitamins and minerals, most notably vitamins A, C, and K, and are also good sources of calcium, potassium, iron, and manganese.

Sautéed Dandelion
Ingredients:
- 3 pounds dandelion greens, tough stems discarded and leaves cut crosswise into 2-inch pieces
- ½ cup extra-virgin olive oil
- 5 large garlic cloves, minced
- ¼ to ½ teaspoon dried hot red pepper flakes
- ½ teaspoon fine sea salt

Dandelion seeds.

Preparation:
1. Cook greens in a 10- to 12-quart pot of boiling salted water, uncovered, until the ribs (midveins) are tender (about 10 minutes).
2. Move to a colander, rinse under cold water, and drain, gently pressing out excess water.
3. Heat oil in a 12-inch heavy skillet over medium heat.
4. Cook garlic and red pepper flakes, stirring until pale golden, about 45 seconds.
5. Increase heat to medium-high. Add greens and sea salt.
6. Sauté until coated with oil and heated through (about 4 minutes).

Tempura Dandelion Flowers

Ingredients:
- 2 cups freshly picked dandelions (never exposed to chemicals)
- Vegetable oil for deep frying
- 1 large egg, cold from the fridge
- 3 tablespoons white rice flour
- Pinch of sea salt
- 4 tablespoons ice cold water

Procedure:
1. Check dandelion blooms for bugs.

2. Heat a saucepan with vegetable oil, not more than three-quarters full, for deep frying. The temperature should be 350°F. Test for the correct temperature with a cube of bread; when it sizzles and rises to the top immediately, it's ready.
3. In a bowl, whisk the egg well. Add the rice flour, salt, and enough ice-cold water to make a thin, runny batter.
4. Dip the dandelion blooms into the batter head first and spoon over batter to cover the green back. Drain excess batter and gently drop head first into the hot oil.

Dandelion flower.

5. Fry for a couple of seconds until golden, flip, and cook the other side for a few seconds more. Remove from the oil with a slotted or mesh spoon and drain on absorbent paper.
6. Sprinkle with salt and/or preferred seasonings and serve immediately.

Notes: Humans have eaten dandelion roots going back at least 25,000 years.

Unlike most root plants that are harvested in the fall, dandelion roots should be harvested in the spring, when they become sweeter.

ELDERBERRY

Elderberry fruits.

Scientific Name: *Sambucus canadensis*
Type of Plant: Flowering deciduous shrub
Description: The oppositely arranged leaves are pinnate with five to nine leaflets. Each leaf is two to thirteen inches long, and the leaflets have serrated margins. The flowers bear large clusters of small white or cream-colored flowers in late spring; these are followed by clusters of small black, blue-black, or red berries (sometimes, but rarely, yellow or white).
Natural Range: The elderberry grows worldwide from temperate to subtropical regions but is more often found in the Northern Hemisphere.
Food Usage: Many cultures produce elderberry and elderflower syrup for cooking. The syrup is also used as a drink or as a flavoring.

Elderberry leaves.

Elderberry plant.

Elderberry Dumplings

Berry Mixture
Ingredients:
- 2 cups elderberries
- ¾ cup sugar
- 1 tablespoon flour
- 2 tablespoons lemon juice
- ¾ cup water

Procedure:
1. Combine all the ingredients.
2. Heat gently in a small pan until liquid has thickened a bit.
3. Keep filling warm while you make the dumplings.

Dumpling Batter
Ingredients:
- ¾ cup flour, sifted
- 1½ teaspoon baking powder
- ½ teaspoon cinnamon
- ½ teaspoon salt
- ¼ cup sugar
- ¼ cup grated lemon peel
- ¼ cup milk
- 1 egg

Procedure:
1. Add baking powder, cinnamon, salt, sugar, and lemon peel to the sifted and measured flour.
2. Mix the milk and the egg in a small bowl
3. Stir wet ingredients into the flour combination until the dough is just blended.
4. Pour the hot berry mixture into a casserole dish
5. Drop in small spoonfuls of the dumpling batter.
6. Bake at 400°F for 25–30 minutes until the pastry balls are lightly browned.
7. Serve the dessert warm with cream or vanilla ice cream.

Elderberry flowers and leaves.

Elderberry Pancake Syrup

Materials:

- ¾ cup dried elderberries
- 3 cups water
- 1 teaspoon ground cinnamon or 1 cinnamon stick
- 1 teaspoon ground cloves or 4 whole cloves
- 1 tablespoon fresh ginger or 1 teaspoon dried ginger
- 1 cup raw honey

Elderberry syrup.

Procedure:

1. Simmer berries and spices in water for about 45 minutes. The liquid should be reduced by half.
2. Drain through a fine mesh strainer. Squeeze liquid out of berries.
3. Add raw honey when liquid is cooled.

Notes: Elderberry syrup is very popular during cold and flu season, which means it is both hard to find in stores and somewhat expensive. Elderberries are easy to grow. If you can get a live branch, it will probably grow just by sticking the cut end into the ground.

Kudzu leaves.

KUDZU

Scientific Name: *Pueraria montana* var. *lobata* (East Asian arrowroot)
Type of Plant: Perennial vine
Description: Kudzu is a climbing, semi-woody vine that is related to peas. Its deciduous leaves are composed of three broad leaflets that are up to four inches across. Individual flowers are purple, fragrant, and hang in long clusters. The seedpods are brown, hairy, and flat. The pods contain three to ten hard seeds.
Natural Range: Native to Japan, kudzu was introduced into the United States in 1876 to control erosion. Kudzu is very common throughout the Southeast along roadsides and disturbed areas.
Food Usage: The leaves, flowers, and roots are edible. The roots contain a starch that has been used as a foodstuff in Asia for hundreds of years. In Vietnam, the root starch is used to flavor pomelo oil and is drunk in the summertime. Kudzu root starch can be used as a substitute for corn starch. The flowers are used to make a jelly that tastes similar to grape jelly, but it is the leaves that we will use in the recipe below.

Invasive kudzu.

Rolled Kudzu Leaves
Ingredients:
- 30 medium-sized young kudzu leaves (gathered from an area free of herbicides used to kill kudzu)
- 1 cup rice
- 1 pound ground lamb or lean beef
- 1 can plus 1 cup diced tomatoes, separated
- ½ teaspoon ground allspice
- Salt and pepper
- 2 teaspoons salt
- 3 cloves garlic, crushed
- Juice of 3 lemons

Kudzu leaves.

Kudzu flowers.

Procedure:

1. Drop leaves into boiling salt water. Boil for 2–3 minutes, while gently stirring to separate leaves. Remove and place on a plate to cool.
2. Cut along stem to middle leaf to remove heavy center.
3. Combine rice, meat, diced tomatoes, allspice, and salt and pepper, and mix well to create stuffing.
4. Fill with 1 teaspoon stuffing and roll in the shape of a cigar.
5. Place parchment paper or aluminum foil in bottom of a large pan so that rolled leaves will not sit directly on the bottom of the pan.
6. Arrange leaf rolls alternately in opposite directions.
7. Pour remaining 1 can diced tomatoes, 2 teaspoons salt, and 3 cloves crushed garlic over the leaves.
8. Press down with an inverted dish and add water to reach dish.
9. Cover pot and cook on medium for 30 minutes.
10. Add lemon juice and cook another 10 minutes.

Kudzu Tea

Ingredients:
- 1 cup kudzu leaves, finely chopped
- 4 cups water
- Honey
- Mint

Kudzu flowers.

Procedure:

1. Simmer kudzu leaves in water for 30 minutes.
2. Drain and serve with honey and a sprig of mint.
3. If you prefer a sweeter tea, add more honey to taste.

Note: Kudzu is thought to take over, and while it is hard to eradicate once established, and the vines grow several feet in a day, it cannot tolerate shade, and does not go deep into wooded areas.

Lamb's quarters flowers.

LAMB'S QUARTERS

Scientific Name: *Chenopodium album*

Type of Plant: Annual

Description: Lamb's quarters is a rapidly growing summer weed that averages three feet tall. The extremely adaptable growth behavior of lamb's quarters enables the plant to grow in almost any environment. Stems are erect and sturdy and are often tinged red or have pink, purple, or yellow stripes.

Natural Range: Lamb's quarters is found at in all inhabited areas of the world except extreme desert climates. It is one of the five most widely distributed plants in the world. It is one of the last weeds to be killed by frost, and its presence is one of the best indicators of good soil.

Food Usage: Lamb's quarters is eaten as a green; however, the flavor is variable due to size of the plant and the growing conditions. They are best eaten when young, because as the leaves mature with age, they gain a greater potency of oxalic acid, which in strong amounts can cause an unpleasant burning sensation in the back of the throat.

Lamb's quarters.

Lamb's Quarters Soup

Ingredients:
- 1 small onion, chopped
- 3 tablespoons butter
- 3 tablespoons flour
- 1½ teaspoons salt
- Pepper
- 3 cups milk
- 2 cups cooked young lamb's quarters, chopped lightly

Procedure:
1. Cook up onion in butter until wilted.
2. Add flour and cook until mixture browns.
3. Season with salt and pepper. Cook for 3 minutes over medium heat.
4. Add milk and lamb's quarters.
5. Heat gently.

Lamb's quarters plant.

Lamb's quarters leaves.

Alternative Usage: Lambs quarter contains saponin, which acts as a mild soap substitute.

Lamb's Quarters Soap Substitute
Ingredients:
- Fresh lamb's quarters roots
- Water

Procedure:
1. Clean fresh roots and mash between two rocks.
2. Rub roots vigorously with a small amount of water to form light suds.

Notes: Lamb's quarters absorbs nitrates readily, so avoid gathering where fertilizer runs off or in other contaminated soil. Also beware of similar plants that have a bad smell. Lamb's quarters does not emit a bad or resinous smell when you crush its leaves between your fingers.

MAYAPPLE

Mayapple plants.

Scientific Name: *Podophyllum peltatum*
Type of Plant: Perennial
Description: Mayapples are woodland plants, typically growing in mature forests in large groups sharing a single root. The stems grow to 10 to 15 inches tall, with umbrella-like leaves. Some stems bear a single leaf and do not flower or fruit, while others produce a pair of leaves with a single flower. The two-inch diameter flower is waxy and whitepetaled with yellow pistils and stamens, and develops into a yellow berry that is the size and shape of a small hen's egg.

Natural Range: The mayapple grows in moist soils in rich woods, thickets, and pastures in Eastern North America from Southern Maine to Florida, and west to Texas and Minnesota.

Food Usage: All parts of the plant, except the ripe fruit, are poisonous. The fully ripe fruit is yellow and feels soft. It can be eaten raw or cooked. It can be made into jams, jellies, or pies. Mayapple seeds and rind are not edible.

Mayapple Jelly Recipe

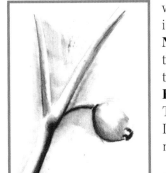

Mayapple fruit.

Ingredients:
- 2 cups mayapple slices
- 3 cups water
- ⅛ cup lemon juice

Mayapple fruit.

- 3½ cups sugar
- 3 ounces liquid fruit pectin

Procedure:

1. Wash ripe mayapples and cut away stem, blossom ends, and any discolored or damaged areas. Remove seeds and rind. Cut fruit into pieces.
2. Place mayapple slices in large kettle with water to cover. Bring to a boil, then simmer until fruit is tender, mashing during cooking.
3. Strain juice through cheesecloth (2 cups fruit should result in at least 1¾ cups juice).
4. Add lemon juice and sugar to strained juice.
5. Bring mixture to a boil, stirring in the liquid fruit pectin.
6. Continue to boil and stir constantly until "jelly stage" is reached.
7. Remove jelly from heat, skim foam from top, and pour into hot, sterilized jelly jars.
8. Seal at once with lid, and process jars in hot water bath. For half pints or pint jars, process for 5 minutes at altitudes from 0 to 1,000 feet; 10 minutes for altitudes from 1,001 to 6,000 feet; and 15 minutes for altitudes above 6,000 feet.

Notes: The ripened fruit is edible in small amounts, but is poisonous when consumed in large amounts. The rhizome, foliage, and roots are also poisonous.

Mayapple plant.

Milk thistle plant.

MILK THISTLE

Scientific Name: *Silybum marianum*

Type of Plant: Annual or biennial

Description: Milk thistle is a stout plant that grows up to one yard tall and has a branched stem. Milk thistle can easily be identified by its uniquely shaped flower and prickly stem. Milk thistle flower heads are light purple in color. They flower from June to August in the Northern Hemisphere or December to February in the Southern Hemisphere.

Natural Range: Milk thistle is grown worldwide, and in some countries is considered an invasive weed.

Food Usage: Milk thistle has been used as food. Personally, I use it to make vegetable rennet for cheese. The roots can be eaten raw or boiled, parboiled, or roasted. The young shoots in spring can be cut down to the root and boiled. The prime time to harvest and peel the stems is before the flowers form. The spiny bracts on the flower head can be eaten like globe artichoke (which it is related to) and the stems (after peeling) can be soaked overnight and stewed.

Milk thistle flowers.

Prepared Milk Thistle Stalks

Ingredients:
- Milk thistle stalk

Procedure:
1. Turn thistle stalk over and make an incision with a knife near the base of the stalk, cutting through the stalk toward the leaves. Do not cut completely through. By cutting the stalk, you can peel the leaves away.
2. Once the thorny leaves are peeled away, scrape out the fiber in the center of the stalk. This leaves a stalk that looks like celery.
3. Cut into smaller segments and enjoy raw with a dip as you would celery stalks, or add to salads, stir-fry, or boil.

Milk Thistle Seed Coffee Substitute

Ingredients:
- Milk thistle seeds
- Water

Procedure:
1. Spread the seeds on a cookie sheet and toast them in the oven at 350°F for 10 minutes.
2. Allow them to return to room temperature, then grind them in a coffee grinder and brew them as you would coffee grounds.

Other Uses for Milk Thistle Seed: The seeds of milk thistle have many uses. You can add whole, raw milk thistle seeds to salads or to your favorite trail mix. If you want to add a protein boost to a smoothie, yogurt, or a shake, you can stir in a tablespoon of ground milk thistle seeds.

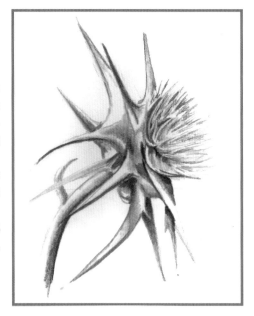

(Above) Milk thistle flower.
(Below) Milk thistle.

MULLEIN

Close-up of mullein leaves show they are soft and furry.

Scientific Name: *Verbascum* is the genus.
Type of Plant: Perennial or biennial
Description: Mullein grows from one and a half to ten feet tall. Young plants start as a dense rosette of leaves at ground level, and send up a tall flowering stem as they grow. The leaves are spirally arranged and densely hairy, although some species of mullein are hairless. The flowers have five symmetrical petals; petal colors include yellow, orange, red-brown, purple, blue, or white. The fruit is a capsule that contains many tiny seeds.
Natural Range: Mullein can be found growing in open fields, waste places, disturbed areas, railway embankments, and similar dry, sunny localities.
Food Usage: The only palatable way to eat mullein is by making a tea. The fine hairs on the leaves make it inedible.

Mullein flowers.

Mullein plant.

(Above) Mullein plant. (Below) Mullein flower.

Mullein Tea

Ingredients:
- 6 large mullein leaves
- 5 cups boiling water
- Honey (optional)

Procedure:
1. Break leaves into small pieces.
2. Add boiling water.
3. Let the tea steep for 5 minutes. Strain through a coffee filter to remove fine hairs.
4. Serve with honey if desired.

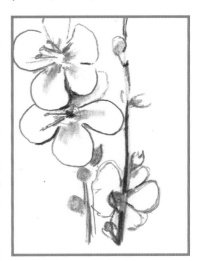

Alternative Usage: While mullein tea is a traditional herbal tea, mullein has another vital use. It is also known as cowboy toilet paper. While I don't feel the need to go into detail with instructions for using a leaf for toiletry purposes, I will say that you should use the leaf in a direction that flows with the hairs and you should test your skin with the leaf because it can cause nausea or contact dermatitis in some people.

Notes: The stalk of the plant is a good drill for use in the hand drill method of friction fire lighting.

Purslane.

PURSLANE

Scientific Name: *Portulaca oleracea*

Type of Plant: Annual

Description: Purslane has smooth, reddish stems that mostly lie on the ground. The stem has alternate leaves that cluster at both the stem ends and joints. The flowers are yellow and have five regular parts and are up to a quarter-inch wide. The flowers may appear regardless of the season depending on rainfall, but they only open for a few hours on sunny mornings.

Natural Range: Purslane grows in orchards, vineyards, crop fields, gardens, roadsides, and other disturbed sites throughout the United States. It can live in compacted soils and is very tolerant of both poor soil and drought conditions due to its taproot and strong secondary roots.

Food Usage: Purslane contains omega-3s and beta-carotene, plus vitamin C in its stems. It tastes similar to spinach and can be substituted for it in most recipes.

Purslane flowers. Credit: Bob Peterson, CC BY 2.0.

Purslane Pesto

Ingredients:

- One large handful of purslane with the stems removed
- ⅔ cup walnuts
- ¼ cup olive oil
- Juice from half a lemon
- 2 teaspoons honey
- Sea salt and pepper

Procedure:

1. Place all ingredients in a food processor and pulse until you can't see any whole leaves.
2. Use it on toasted bread, pizza, or with pasta.

Purslane flowers.

Purslane.

Cucumber and Purslane Soup

Ingredients:
- 2½ cups roughly chopped cucumbers
- 1 green tomato, roughly chopped
- 1 medium young onion
- 3 young garlic cloves, peeled
- ½ cup purslane leaves and tips
- ½ fresh green chili pepper
- ¾ cup Greek yogurt
- 2 teaspoons sherry vinegar
- ½ teaspoon sugar
- Large pinch of salt
- ½ stale pita bread, broken into pieces (or ¼ cup ground almonds)
- 2 tablespoons extra virgin olive oil

Procedure:
1. Put all ingredients into a blender and blend until smooth.
2. Add additional salt, sugar, and water to reach the desired texture and flavor.
3. Chill, and serve in cups.

SHEPHERD'S PURSE

Shepherd's purse.

Scientific Name: *Capsella bursa-pastoris*

Type of Plant: Annual

Description: Shepherd's purse is named from its triangular, purse-like pods. The plant is a small annual plant related to mustard. Unlike most flowering plants, shepherd's purse flowers year-round, making it capable of producing several generations a year. Shepherd's purse grows from a rosette of lobed leaves on the ground. A foot-long stem grows from this base. The flowers are small and white and produce heart-shaped seed pods.

Natural Range: Shepherd's purse is native to Eastern Europe and Asia Minor, but is naturalized through the world. Its ability to rapidly reseed causes it to be considered a weed in many places. It grows on disturbed soil, in untended meadows and lawns, and along roadsides and trails.

Food Usage: Shepherd's purse is used as a very mild mustard green. It contains vitamins C, A, and K, some protein, as well as sulfur, calcium, iron, potassium, and sodium. The greens shrink about 75 percent when cooked.

Shepherd's purse flowers and seed pods.

Shepherd's Purse Butter

Ingredients:
- 10 capers
- ½ cup chopped shepherd's purse leaves
- 3½ ounces butter
- 1 garlic clove
- 2 anchovies
- 1 hard-boiled egg
- 1 egg yolk
- 1½ tablespoons vinegar
- Salt and pepper to taste

Procedure:
1. Rinse the capers and wash the greens carefully.
2. Process all the ingredients together in a blender.

This compound butter is really good on fish.

(Above) Shepherd's purse.
(Below) Shepherd's purse flower.

Shepherd's Purse Stir-Fry

Ingredients:
- 3 cups shepherd's purse
- 1 tablespoon corn oil
- 1 garlic clove, minced or pressed

Procedure:
1. Soak the shepherd's purse leaves in cold water for one minute, then drain. Repeat twice more and set aside.
2. Heat oil on high in a nonstick frying pan. When bubbles start to form, add the garlic and stir.
3. Once the garlic has lightly browned, add the shepherd's purse. Stir gently for 1 minute. Remove from heat and serve.

STINGING NETTLE

Stinging nettle close-up—look at the hairs.

Scientific Name: *Urtica dioica*
Type of Plant: Perennial
Description: Stinging nettle has many hollow stinging hairs on the leaves and stems. These hairs act like hypodermic needles that inject histamine and other chemicals (including acetyl-choline, serotonin, moroidin, leukotrienes, and formic acid) causing a stinging sensation when contacted by humans and other animals. The nettle grows three to seven feet tall during the summer, but dies down to the ground during the winter. The leaves are one to six inches long and grow oppositely on a wiry stem. The leaves have a strongly serrated edge. The numerous flowers are small with a green or brown tint.

Stinging nettle is a plant that I have seeded into the land behind my back fence. I have done this because of the usefulness of the plant, but I have to admit I did run into some trouble with my neighbors when I was deciding what types of plants to seed in a permacul-ture–type food forest.

Natural Range: Nettles are native to Europe, Asia, Northern Africa, as well as Western North America. In the United States, it is found in every state except for Hawaii. It grows best in places with high annual rainfall.

Food Usage: While the stinging nettle has fine hairs on the leaves and stems that inject painful chemicals into the skin when touched, it is a wild edible with several uses. Nettles are best eaten as a cooked green, as cooking destroys the painful chemicals. Be sure to wear gloves when you are harvesting stinging nettle. You can also use nettles for any baked recipe that calls for spinach.

Stinging nettle.

Nettle Greens

Ingredients:
- 2 or 3 handfuls stinging nettle leaves
- ¼ cup Parmesan cheese
- Salt and pepper

Procedure:
1. Rinse nettles in a colander then toss in a pot with lid, leaving water on the leaves.
2. Cook on medium high heat 2–4 minutes or until tender.
3. Sprinkle with Parmesan and salt and pepper.

Alternative Usage: Stinging nettle works just like thistle to coagulate milk, so you can make cheese. As with thistle, this vegetarian rennet will impart a bitter flavor to aged cheese so it is not recommended for cheeses that require an aging process longer than two months.

Stinging nettle flower.

Nettle Rennet

Ingredients:
- 2 pounds fresh nettle leaves
- 4 cups water
- Salt

Nettle tea is good for the hair.

Procedure:
1. Rinse fresh leaves.
2. Fill a large pot with water.
3. Add the clean leaves. Add more water if needed to just cover the nettle leaves.
4. Bring the water and leaves to a light boil. Reduce heat, cover, and simmer 30 minutes.
5. Add 1 heaping tablespoon of sea salt to the pot. Stir gently to dissolve.
6. Place a colander inside a large bowl. Line the colander with one layer of clean cheesecloth.
7. Pour nettles into colander.
8. Collect the water by draining until leaves stop dripping.

The liquid drained from the nettle leaves is the liquid nettle rennet. It can be used in amounts of one cup of nettle rennet to one gallon of warmed milk. If kept cold and away from light, it will keep for a few weeks.

Notes: If you don't grasp the nettle tightly (or use gloves) it can irritate the skin and cause pain.

Stinging nettle.

Stinging nettle *hurts*!

WILD BERGAMOT

A field of wild bergamot. The leaves can grow mold, so be careful when harvesting them.

Scientific Name: *Monarda fistulosa*
Type of Plant: Herbaceous perennial
Description: *Monarda fistulosa* grows from slender creeping rhizomes, thus commonly occurring in large clumps. The plants are typically up to three feet tall, with a few erect branches. Its leaves are about two to three inches long, lance-shaped, and toothed. Its compact flower clusters are solitary at the ends of branches. Each cluster is about one and a half inches long, containing about 20 to 50 flowers. Wild bergamot often grows in rich soils in dry fields, thickets, and clearings, usually on limy soil. The plants generally flower from June to September.
Natural Range: Wild bergamot is a wildflower in the mint family (Lamiaceae) and is widespread and abundant as a native plant in much of North America. It ranges from Canada, south to Georgia, Texas, Arizona, Idaho, and Northeastern Washington state. It is found in dry to medium moisture, well-drained soils in full sun to part shade and tolerates somewhat poor soils and some drought.

Wild bergamot flower head.

Food Usage: Wild bergamot is similar to mint; it is best as a flavoring, and it makes a decent tea. Dried, the leaves will have a concentrated flavor, reminiscent of oregano pizza spice (wild bergamot is sometimes called wild oregano). The dried flowers will have a softer flavor, and while they are still usable, they are most potent when fresh. Fresh flowers are excellent sprinkled over a salad or used as a garnish with chicken, fish, and pork.

Wild Bergamot Chocolate Cookies

Ingredients:
- 1½ cups lavender bergamot tips (pluck the top few inches of the plant; you want the leaves and the tender, not woody, stems)
- ¾ cup granulated sugar
- 1¼ cups unsalted butter, cubed, at room temperature
- ¾ cup brown sugar
- 2 eggs
- 1¾ cups flour
- 1¼ cups cocoa powder, sifted so that it is not lumpy
- 2 teaspoons baking soda

Bees and hummingbirds are attracted to wild bergamot.

Procedure:
1. Coarsely grind the bergamot tips and granulated sugar together in a food processor or blender, until the sugar turns green and there are no more distinguishable plant pieces.
2. Cream butter with brown sugar and the wild bergamot sugar. Blend in the eggs, one at a time.
3. Combine the flour, cocoa powder, and baking soda. Add the dry ingredient mixture to the butter mixture, and slowly mix until incorporated.
4. Wrap the dough in plastic wrap and chill for 30 minutes.
5. Scoop the dough using an ice cream scoop into 1½-inch balls. Place the dough balls on a baking sheet lined with parchment paper, 1 inch apart.
6. Bake at 350°F for 5 minutes. Rotate the tray and bake another 3 minutes, or until lightly brown.

Rosehip Bergamot Jelly
Ingredients:
- 8 cups rosehips
- 4 cups apple juice
- ½ cup wild bergamot leaves and flower petals
- 4 cups sugar
- 1 package pectin

Procedure:
1. Bring rosehips and apple juice to a boil. Remove from heat and strain out the rosehips.
2. Add wild bergamot, sugar, and pectin. Stir to dissolve. Reduce heat and let simmer until the flavors have fully blended.
3. Pour into sterilized jars.

Notes: Wild bergamot is also known as bee balm, and it is very attractive to bees, butterflies, and hummingbirds. Many people, the author included, plant some in their gardens to help attract bees and other pollinators.

WILD GOOSEBERRY

Wild gooseberries. The green fruits turn reddish purple as they ripen.

Scientific Name: *Ribes missouriense*
Type of Plant: Deciduous shrub
Description: Wild gooseberry, is a dense, rounded, deciduous shrub with upright-spreading to arching stems. It typically grows to two to four feet tall and as wide, but may rise to as much as six feet. The gooseberry is noted for having showy spring flowers, edible fruits, palmately lobed leaves, and stout thorns.

Drooping, trumpet-shaped, greenish-white to white flowers bloom in spring. Flowers appear solitary or in small clusters of two to three. This shrub requires both male and female plants for fruit production. Pollinated female flowers give way to spherical, tart, juicy, green fruits (up to one-half-inch diameter) that ripen to purple in summer.

Natural Range: Wild gooseberry is a prickly, multiple stemmed shrub native to the North Central United States. Scattered populations have been found farther east. It is typically found in dry rocky woods, thickets, woodland borders, and grazed areas.

Food Usage: Many like to eat the edible ripe fruit raw, but it is also made into gooseberry pie and jam.

Gooseberry Rice Lettuce Wraps

Ingredients:
- 1 cup uncooked rice (3 cups cooked)
- Water
- 1 pint gooseberries
- 1 cup sugar
- 6 tablespoons olive oil
- 3 tablespoons lemon juice
- 1 tablespoon soy sauce
- Lettuce leaves

Wild gooseberry jam.

Procedure:
1. Boil a medium pot of water.
2. Rinse the rice until the water runs clear. Add rice to boiling water and cook according to package directions. When cooked, rinse cold water over the rice and drain.
3. Coarsely chop the gooseberries. Sprinkle with sugar to enrich the flavor without making them too sweet.
4. Beat the oil and lemon juice until quite thick, add the soy sauce, and beat again until well blended.
5. When ready to serve, place the flaky rice on lettuce leaves. Cover the rice with chopped berries. Dress with the oil mixture.

Gooseberry Jam

This particular recipe is an historical one published in *The Saturday Evening Post* on July 12, 1856.

Ingredients:
- 1 pound red gooseberries
- 1 pound brown sugar
- Clean jars

Procedure:
1. Pick and clean red gooseberries.
2. Boil them (by themselves) for 20 minutes, skimming frequently.
3. Add brown sugar. Boil for half an hour.
4. Skim, and pour jam into jars.

Notes: The gooseberry is an alternate host for white pine blister rust, which can cause serious damage to American white pines. Gooseberry cultivation is thus illegal in some areas of the United States, and quarantines are in place to help control this disease.

WILD ROSE

Wild rose flower and leaves.

Scientific Name: *Rosa canina*
Type of Plant: Deciduous shrub
Description: Wild rose is a thorny climbing shrub, it has curved spines to gain a purchase as it weaves in between other shrubs and uses them to support its growth. The flowers are large, pink or white, and have five petals with a faint, sweet smell. The leaves are made up of two to three smaller leaflets. The fruits are red oval-shaped hips that form in small clusters, and each hip contains many seeds.
Natural Range: The wild rose is native to Europe, Northwest Africa, and Western Asia. American colonists naturalized wild rose so early in our country's history that many Americans believe it to be a native plant.
Food Usage: Both rose hips and rose petals are edible. Rose hips also have a bit of the tartness of crab apples and are a great source of vitamin C.

Wild Rose Petal Jam

Ingredients:

- 4 large handfuls wild rose petals
- 1 lemon, juiced
- 1 pint water
- 1 pound sugar
- 1 packet pectin
- Sterilized jars

Procedure:

1. Add rose petals, lemon juice, and water to a pan and simmer on low heat for 15 minutes, stirring periodically.
2. Add the sugar and continue cooking on low heat until the sugar has dissolved.
3. Strain and discard the petals (or keep them if you want).
4. Add a packet of pectin and bring to a rolling boil, keeping a close eye on it for signs that it is reaching the setting point.
5. Take off the heat and test the jam on a cold plate and see if it crinkles when you drag your finger through it.
6. Carefully put into sterilized jars.

Rose Hip Vinaigrette

Ingredients:

- ¼ cup dried whole or cut-and-sifted rose hips
- 1 cup water
- 2 tablespoons vinegar
- ¼ teaspoon powdered yellow mustard
- 1½ teaspoons minced fresh oregano
- 1½ teaspoons minced fresh basil
- ⅛ teaspoon freshly ground black pepper
- 3–4 tablespoons extra-virgin olive oil (or a combination of olive and walnut oils)

Rosehips.

Wild rose.

- ½–1 tablespoon sugar (or ⅛–¼ teaspoon powdered stevia extract or 3–4 drops liquid stevia extract)
- 1 clove garlic, minced (optional)

Procedure:

1. Simmer the rose hips and water, covered, in a nonreactive saucepan for 5 minutes.
2. Let stand off heat for 5 minutes.
3. Strain, pressing the pulp with the back of a spoon.
4. Combine the strained liquid with the remaining ingredients in a jar with a tight-fitting lid. Shake vigorously over the sink.
5. Use the dressing immediately or refrigerate it for up to 2 weeks.

Notes: During World War II, local schoolchildren harvested rose hips to eat during rationing; the hairy seeds were kept, dried, powdered, and made into an "itch" powder used to tease other children. Obviously this type of bullying isn't an appropriate use of foraging knowledge.

Flowering wild rose (dog rose) bush.

WILD STRAWBERRY

Wild strawberry plant. Courtesy USFDA.

Scientific Name: *Fragaria virginiana*
Type of Plant: Herbaceous perennial
Description: This species of wild strawberry is four to seven inches tall. Its leaves are trifoliate (it is three-leaved), and the leaflets are up to two and a half inches long and one and a half inches across; they are oval in shape and coarsely toothed along their middle to outer margins. The tips of leaflets are rounded, while their bottoms are either wedge-shaped or rounded. The upper leaflet surface is medium to dark green. The lower leaflet surface is hairy; fine hairs are most likely to occur along the bases of central veins, but they may occur elsewhere along the lower surface.
Natural Range: Its natural range is confined to North America, in the United States (including Alaska) and Canada. The wild strawberry grows in prairies, meadows, open woodlands, woodland borders, savannas, limestone glades, roadsides, and areas along railroads. It is able to tolerate competition from taller plants because it develops early in the spring.
Food Usage: Many people just eat the berries, but the greens can also be enjoyed.

Wild Strawberry Spinach Salad
Ingredients:
- 2 tablespoons sesame seeds
- 1 tablespoon poppy seeds

Wild strawberries are smaller than ones you find in a grocery store.

- ½ cup sugar
- ½ cup olive oil
- ¼ cup distilled white vinegar
- ¼ teaspoon paprika
- ¼ teaspoon Worcestershire sauce
- 1 tablespoon minced onion
- 10 ounces fresh spinach, rinsed, dried, and torn into bite-size pieces
- 1 quart wild strawberries, cleaned, hulled, and sliced
- ¼ cup blanched and slivered almonds

Procedure:

1. In a medium bowl, whisk together the sesame seeds, poppy seeds, sugar, olive oil, vinegar, paprika, Worcestershire sauce, and onion.
2. Cover and chill for one hour.
3. In a large bowl, combine the spinach, strawberries, and almonds. Pour dressing over salad, and toss.
4. Refrigerate 10 to 15 minutes before serving.

Whole Wheat Wild Strawberry Muffins

Ingredients:
- Nonstick cooking spray
- 1 cup wild strawberries, washed, hulled, and chopped into small pieces
- 2 eggs
- 1 cup plain yogurt
- ¼ cup butter, melted
- 1 teaspoon vanilla
- 2 cups whole wheat flour
- ½ cup packed brown sugar
- 1½ teaspoons baking soda

Procedure:
1. Preheat oven to 400°F.
2. Grease muffin tin with cooking spray, or use paper liners.
3. Place strawberries in small bowl. Add eggs, yogurt, melted butter, and vanilla. Mix well.

A patch of wild strawberries. Credit: Joshua Mayer, CC BY-SA 2.0.

4. In a medium bowl, add together whole wheat flour, brown sugar, and baking soda. Mix well.
5. Add strawberry mixture to flour mixture. Mix well until ingredients are wet. Do not over mix.
6. Spoon the muffin batter into muffin tins, about 2/3 full. Bake for 20 minutes or until tops are golden brown.

Notes: *Fragaria virginiana* was one of two wild strawberries that were hybridized to make the modern domesticated strawberry.

On January 4, 1996, the Nebraska Supreme Court handed down a decision that affects anyone buying strawberries in a store in that state. In an effort to avoid confusion, the court declared that a store could not sell strawberries by weight and by volume in the same store at the same time. If the store desired, they could sell the strawberries by weight one day, and by volume the next.

SUGGESTED READING

I really like the Peterson Field Guides, as well as the Audubon Society guides. I find that identification guides with full color photographs are highly valuable for identification, with books on edibility and usage better for learning what to do with the plants identified.

USEFUL FIELD GUIDES:

The Scout's Guide to Wild Edibles: Learn How to Forage, Prepare & Eat 40 Wild Foods by Mike Krebill (St. Lynn's Press, 2016)

A Peterson Field Guide to Edible Wild Plants: Eastern and Central North America by Lee Peterson (Houghton Mifflin Harcourt, 1977)

A Peterson Field Guide to Medicinal Plants and Herbs of Eastern and Central North America, Third Edition by Steven Foster & James A. Duke (Houghton Mifflin Harcourt, 2014)

Plant Identification Terminology: An Illustrated Glossary by James G. Harris and Melinda Woolf Harris (Spring Lake, 2001)

American Horticultural Society Encyclopedia of Plants and Flowers by Christopher Brickell (DK, 2011)

Trees of North America: A Guide to Field Identification by C. Frank Brockman (Golden Guides from St. Martin's Press, 2001)

National Audubon Society Field Guide to North American Trees: Eastern Region (Alfred A. Knopf, 1980)

The Forager's Harvest: A Guide to Identifying, Harvesting, and Preparing Edible Wild Plants by Samuel Thayer (Forager's Harvest Press, 2006)

The North American Guide to Common Poisonous Plants and Mushrooms by Nancy J. Turner and Patrick von Aderkas (Timber Press, 2009)

Rosemary Gladstar's Medicinal Herbs: A Beginner's Guide by Rosemary Gladstar (Storey Publishing, 2012)

Nature's Garden: A Guide to Identifying, Harvesting, and Preparing Edible Wild Plants by Samuel Thayer (Forager's Harvest Press, 2010)

Tom Brown's Guide to Wild Edible and Medicinal Plants by Tom Brown Jr. (Berkley, 1986)

The Illustrated Guide to Edible Wild Plants by Department of the Army (Lyons Press, 2003)

Edible Wild Plants: A North American Field Guide to Over 200 Natural Foods by Thomas Elias and Peter Dykeman (Sterling, 2009)

The Herbal Medicine-Maker's Handbook: A Home Manual by James Green (Crossing Press, 2000)

Incredible Wild Edibles: 36 Plants That Can Change Your Life by Samuel Thayer (Foragers Harvest, 2018)

Idiot's Guides: Foraging by Mark Vorderbruggen (Alpha, Penguin Random House, 2015)

Northeast Foraging: 120 Wild and Flavorful Edibles from Beach Plums to Wineberries by Leda Meredith (Timber Press, 2014)

Midwest Foraging: 115 Wild and Flavorful Edibles from Burdock to Wild Peach by Lisa Rose (Timber Press, 2015)

Pacific Northwest Foraging: 120 Wild and Flavorful Edibles from Alaska Blueberries to Wild Hazelnuts by Douglas Deur (Timber Press, 2014)

California Foraging: 120 Wild and Flavorful Edibles from Evergreen Huckleberries to Wild Ginger by Judith Larner Lowry (Timber Press, 2014)

Southwest Foraging: 117 Wild and Flavorful Edibles from Barrel Cactus to Wild Oregano by John Slattery (Timber Press, 2016)

Mountain States Foraging: 115 Wild and Flavorful Edibles from Alpine Sorrel to Wild Hops by Briana Wiles (Timber Press, 2016)

Southeast Foraging: 120 Wild and Flavorful Edibles from Angelica to Wild Plums by Chris Bennett (Timber Press, 2015)

Florida's Edible Wild Plants: A Guide to Collecting and Cooking by Peggy Lantz (Seaside Publishing, 2014)

Backyard Foraging: 65 Familiar Plants You Didn't Know You Could Eat by Ellen Zachos (Storey Publishing, 2013)

Wild Edibles: A Practical Guide to Foraging, with Easy Identification of 60 Edible Plants and 67 Recipes by Sergei Boutenko (North Atlantic Books, 2013)

Midwest Medicinal Plants: Identify, Harvest, and Use 109 Wild Herbs for Health and Wellness by Lisa Rose (Timber Press, 2017)

Ancestral Plants: A Primitive Skills Guide to Important Edible, Medicinal, and Useful Plants of the Northeast, Volume 1 by Arthur Haines (Anaskimin, 2010)

Wild Berries & Fruits Field Guide series by Teresa Marrone (Adventure Keen Publications, from 2009 to 2018)

ABOUT THE AUTHOR

David Nash is a dedicated prepper that involves self-reliance and disaster resilience in every portion of his life. Tired of having to wade through Internet misinformation to find out successful methods, he began documenting his journey to learn what does and does not work as he helps his family become better prepared for life's challenges.

His work involves a popular YouTube channel, website, and nonfiction books dedicated to DIY solutions for prepper problems. You can find David online at www.tngun.com.

Other Skyhorse Publishing works by David Nash:

52 Prepper Projects
52 Unique Techniques for Stocking Food for Preppers
52 Prepper's Projects for Parents and Kids
Prepper's Guide to Foraging, First Edition
Basic Survival: A Beginner's Guide
Handguns for Self Defense